DISCARD

THE LAST OF THE
MAASAI

THE LAST OF THE
MAASAI

Mohamed Amin · Duncan Willetts
John Eames
Foreword by Elspeth Huxley

Camerapix Publishers International
NAIROBI

Acknowledgements
The publishers would like to thank Naomi Kipuny for her invaluable help in
verifying and clarifying details of Maasai custom and tradition; also Helen Van
Houten, Donna Klumpp, Daniel Stiles and Mary Anne Fitzgerald for advice
and suggestions.

First published 1987 by
Camerapix Publishers International
PO Box 45048
Nairobi, Kenya

Second impression 1994
Third impression 2000
Fourth impression 2004

© Camerapix 1987

ISBN 1-904722-13-X

This book was designed and produced by
Camerapix Publishers International
PO Box 45048
Nairobi, Kenya

Design: Craig Dodd

Printed in Singapore.

*Preceding pages — Half title: Shaven-haired moran awaits entry into the
ranks of the elders;*
Pages 2-3: Maasai homesteads;
Page 4: Young moran wears eye-catching ruff;
*Page 5: Bondsmen for life —: 'brothers in circumcision' forge inseparable
links; each male generation progresses together through each ritual
graduation of Maasai life until death;*
Pages 6-7: Sundown at Lake Magadi as the herd-boy drives home the goats;
*Title page: Maasai guarding cattle in Amboseli, believe that Enkai, God,
gave all the cattle in the world to them;*
*Contents pages: Dust rises as the hooves of the Maasai herd intermingle
with wild plains game.*

Contents

Foreword by Elspeth Huxley

Ever since white men came to eastern Africa, they have been having an unhappy kind of love affair with the Maasai people. Unhappy, because admiration and exasperation have been almost equally blended in their feelings towards these handsome, arrogant and stubborn tribesmen.

Almost, if not quite, alone among the tribes of eastern Africa, the Maasai have turned their backs upon the prizes and temptations offered by the West. The great majority of other African peoples have, after an initial period of suspicious hesitation, grasped at those offerings with both hands: at western medicine and education and, after a certain lapse of time, at western technology, the open sesame to that glittering goal, a higher standard of living. They have set their feet on the path to the consumer society.

Not the Maasai. For a long time, it is true, there have been schools and hospitals in Maasailand; there are university graduates, professors, Ministers of State – even a lady who in 1970 became the first Maasai woman to graduate from Nairobi University. But, by and large, nearly 70 years of colonial rule and attempted persuasion, followed by more than 25 years of African rule and attempted persuasion, have failed to do more than dent the fabric of custom and tradition. Almost within sight of Nairobi's tower blocks and traffic jams, the Maasai have continued to practise their ancient rituals and ceremonies; they have continued to maintain their age-set structure with its warrior caste of haughty, swift and predatory *moran* – storm troopers or commandos of the tribal world.

For several centuries, Maasai warriors had dominated much of eastern Africa by force of arms. They disdained permanent settlements, pens and trousers, tillers of the soil, a peaceful way of life. They loved the sword and spurned the ploughshare. Their cattle were their life. The moran's pride and duty was to protect their fathers' herds and to capture other people's – which, according to their folklore, rightly belonged to them in any case, since their God had given all the cattle in the world to the Maasai. This belief does not accord with peaceful progress in a properly administered country, whether the administrators are black or white. The same note of exasperation with the Maasai's refusal to conform that was sounded in the reports of early colonial officials is echoed by today's United Nations agencies bent on introducing schemes of range management, water conservation and the like.

Exasperation with Maasai obduracy has been balanced by the admiration these nomads have so often won from people of other races. In colonial days, there was a disease known as 'Maasai-itis' to which district officers, especially young ones, sometimes succumbed. In its advanced stages the victim was said to shake, quiver and even froth at the mouth, as moran were wont to do when working themselves up to battle pitch. Before that stage was reached, it was considered advisable

Opposite: Blowing the horn of the greater kudu used to summon the morans to gather for the unoto *ceremony.*

to post that officer to a non-Maasai district. The leader of the white settlers, Lord Delamere, was so enamoured of the Maasai that when they stole his cattle, as they often did, he refused to prosecute, and even applauded the cunning tricks they got up to when transferring cattle from his ownership to theirs. No other Kenyan people, so far as I know, have won this kind of respect.

On what was it based? The answer most generally given was courage. Maasai moran were brave. When they surrounded a marauding lion, then closed in upon it and finally speared it to death, they displayed great individual fearlessness. As well as being brave, these warriors were often beautiful, because their bodies were lithe, muscular, and perfectly controlled.

Many Europeans also envied the Maasai their apparent freedom, their nomadic way of life uncluttered by possessions, their sexual freedom: an existence regulated by the rhythms of the seasons. And especially they envied, perhaps unconsciously, the comradeship of the age-set – that band of brothers circumcised at the same time – which was unbreakable and knew no bounds. When a man had passed through the *eunoto* ceremony that entitled him to marry and become a junior elder, he was permitted to sleep with the wife of any of his comrades if he so desired. A Maasai woman did not marry just one man, she married a whole age-set. Sexual jealousy between members of an age-set was disallowed, if not perhaps entirely unknown.

And yet, despite all this cultural tenacity, change, like a stain of acid, has seeped in to corrode the foundations of the tribal mores. First the suppression of inter-tribal warfare and then the enforcement of law and order destroyed the purpose of the moran, and the introduction of a western legal system removed power from the elders. Today, even greater pressures are at work, and a good deal more quickly. The African governments who took over from colonial rule have as their avowed aim the abolition of tribal distinctions and the blending of them all, Bantu or Nilotic, into one united people. Maasai tribal pride, Maasai customs, Maasai separateness must go. Adaptation, as we all know, is the price of survival. The dinosaurs did not adapt and they did not survive.

The Maasai and their flocks and herds have for long shared the East African savannah with the great herds of game without attempting to destroy them. Now that situation is changing fast, or has already changed. Schemes of range management launched by international agencies, large-scale wheat-growing projects, and the invasion of their country by land-hungry small-scale cultivators are pressing in upon the Maasai, depriving them of resources essential to the nomadic pattern of their lives and forcing them into alien moulds. How much longer can their way of life survive?

Following page: Ostrich-feather finery of the moran's full-dress uniform is reserved for important ceremonies like the graduation of the warriors, eunoto; in the past it was a symbol of terror for cattle raiders.

John Eames's narrative does not answer the question. He gives us the facts as he sees them, and as they are seen by some Maasai who have, as it were, defected to the West, and leaves us to make up our own minds. It is significant that he suggests, with many Maasai, that the next *eunoto* ceremony, the crux of Maasai custom and the tie that binds the tribe, may be the last ever to be held. But the Maasai will still be there: and adaptation is not impossible. Mr Eames ends on a note of hope. He describes the work of a Roman Catholic mission in the Loita Hills where Father Voschaar and his fellow priests have built dams, bred up cattle of superior quality, improved pastures, and are slowly, gently, without coercion or the imposition of grandiose ideas, arousing the interest of the people, even their cooperation, as so many have tried to do before and failed. They are attempting to build a bridge, a simple one of logs and twine rather than of steel and concrete, between the old and the new. Can they, and others with the same approach, succeed? That is the question. Time is running out.

Meanwhile, the Maasai have a new prayer. It asks their God, *Enkai*, to 'give us the strength to do the work that we have started here' – here being the ranch implanted into Maasailand by the Fathers – which will grow and thrive 'like the *oreteti* tree that is green even in times of drought'.

SUDAN

ETHIOPIA

ZAIRE

Lake Turkana

SOMALIA

UGANDA

Rift Valley

KENYA

Lake Victoria

▲ Mt Kenya

Naivasha

Wuasinkishu

Narok

Damat

Lake Naivasha

RWANDA

Siria

Purko

Keekonyokie

Nairobi

Kitui

Machakos

Loodokilani

Kaputiei

Liotai

Laitayiok

Dalalekutuk

Salei

Matapato

Lake Natron

Kisongo

Laitokitok

BURUNDI

Serenget

Sikirari

▲ Mt Kilimanjaro

Voi

Lake Eyasi

Lake Manyara

Mombasa

MAASAILAND

Simanjiro

Kisongo

TANZANIA

Moipo

ZAIRE

Dar-Es-Salaam

Indian Ocean

ZAMBIA

Scale in Miles

0   50   100   150

MALAWI

MOZAMBIQUE

Opposite: Waiting in an acacia grove after their ritual head shaving, new elders carry wooden staves as symbolic spears for their parade through the village, enkang, of their parents.

Below: Lion-mane head-dress is a symbol of the warrior elite. The right to wear it is earned by the moran who takes the brunt of the beast's charge – or delivers the fatal thrust. Now that lion hunting is banned, some award the mane head-dress to their bravest brothers.

Opposite: Following circumcision, initiates into manhood learn the arts of survival in the wild in small, informal troops of 'cadets', a necessary preliminary to induction as a moran.

Below: Striding boldly through the village of their parents, moran leave for a walk-about.

Opposite: Senior Maasai elders enjoy the veneration of the entire community, and a life of comparative ease. But as members of the council of elders, **enkiguena**, *they make all the major decisions affecting the community. Below: Close-up of venerable elder.*

Overleaf: Fragile grasslands suffer erosion from over-grazing and periodic drought when lean and hungry herds reflect the cyclic rise and fall of Maasai fortune.

*pposite: Elongated ear lobes, hung with beaded and
etal ornaments, form a major focus for jewellery for
th Maasai men and women. When they are very
ung, wooden plugs are inserted to stretch the slit
be.*

*Overleaf: Elaborate coiffure of the Maasai moran, en-
chadai, is his main conceit. These Beau Brummels of
the bush each favour their own styling, often plaited
and smeared liberally with fat.*

*elow: Smiling moran celebrate their elevation to
nior elders. Now they can choose wives, own
ttle, and pursue a less nomadic existence.*

1

ORIGINS

The Maasai warrior is picturesque. He wears a short toga, anything from pink to the colour of dried blood, flapped open in the breeze to show athlete's legs like oiled rope. A long lion spear may be missing, banned by the Kenya Government. But he wears a Roman short sword called *ol alem* and carries a stick or *orinka*, knobkerrie.

He still calls himself a warrior – *ol morani*. His face and long plaited hair are smeared with red ochre and animal fat. He is a century out of time – and out of place – in his own tribal land on a ridge above Nairobi.

No one knows where the Maasai came from. Somewhere north along the Nile – or maybe beyond, further east. In this theory, like the Falasha of western Ethiopia, the Maasai are Jewish: a long lost tribe of Israel.

The idea arose at the turn of the century from a German colonial administrator in the Kilimanjaro district of what was then northern Tanganyika. Captain Moritz Merker was the first of a legion of Maasai watchers, writing volumes of meticulous notes on their life style.

But though the quality of his observation was never argued, the notion of the original Maasai as Israelites is too far-fetched for most academics. There were one or two notable exceptions; a couple of German professors who found a Semitic trace in the Maasai – or *Maa* – language, beliefs and customs.

But this line of research was undeveloped then, so the Merker theory rests mainly and contentiously on folk stories he collected from old men of the Kisonko section around Kilimanjaro. He wrote it down in great detail, all close to the Old Testament main events – creation, flood, commandments, and so on – but with interesting adaptations in the Maasai idiom. In some instances he tracked these back to Babylonian mythology.

A scholarly review of Merker's work from a Professor Wilhelm Schmidt in the 1930s was 'cautiously supportive'. Schmidt concluded that the unread, unsung soldier had touched 'on matters which date back to the original link between the Semites and Hamites' – between the western Arab lands and north-east Africa.

It is also significant that *Enkai*, the sole God of the Maasai, is a Jehovah figure who clearly predated the Christian missionaries in East Africa.

Even so, the Hebrew connection is generally debunked, starting with Merker's contemporary in British East Africa – a Maasailand administrator by the name of A.C. Hollis.

He argued, not unreasonably, that if the Maasai had originated in the region of the Upper Nile, they must have had early contact with the ancient Coptic Christians of Ethiopia. Hence the genesis of Merker's tales of the old men of the Kisonko, warped and 'localised' in the telling over the centuries.

Sir Charles Eliot, Britain's first colonial commissioner to East Africa, located the origins of the Maasai no further north than Sudan, around the old caravan stop of Gondokoro. This much is certain, he said, based on a 'triple bond of resemblance with the Sudanese Bari and Latuka peoples in physique, language and culture'.

For Sir Charles, the Maasai were a mixed race representing a fusion of the Negro with some 'superior type which we must confess to be unknown, though the neighbourhood of Egypt and Abyssinia offers support for many hypotheses'. A successor, Sir Harry Johnson of Uganda, said this 'superiority' was from Hamitic genes taken in from women captured after battles with the Galla of the north-east coastal region. He classified the Maasai as 'Nilo-Hamitic', which stuck for decades until recent African scholars objected to the inference of Caucasian or 'white' blood in people they insist are entirely native.

Probably the first European report on the Maasai was from a German Lutheran pastor, Johann Krapf, who set up a mission in 1848 at the village of Rabai, just outside Mombasa. He reported they were busy with a 'useless and savage civil war' throughout the middle years of the 19th century.

In a scholarly book, he broke the tribe down into two halves – the Maasai proper and the defeated sections grouped under the name 'Kwavi'. And it was these demoralised and 'degenerate' sections, according to Krapf, that gave his more favoured Maasai 'a bad name' for constantly beating up the Bantu tribes around Kilimanjaro and the Taita Hills close to the coast.

Krapf insisted the Maasai tried to stop the 'Kwavi' marauding in what he described as a 'humane police action' on behalf of the weaker, indigenous African tribes. But he wasn't convincing, and just who were the villains of the 19th century is still the subject of academic debate.

An English missionary, the Reverend Charles New, was among the first Europeans to have direct contact with the Maasai and for him they were, without question, the 'congenital killers of the Dark Interior'. He and a colleague, the Reverend Thomas Wakefield, sent reports back to England which added to what was already established in the popular mind about Africa, after the earlier sagas of Livingstone and Stanley.

Wakefield was commissioned to lead an expedition into the Maasai heartland by the Royal Geographical Society. But it was put off, with the Society eventually sending out a 29-year-old Scotsman, Joseph Thomson, with a brief to march through hostile Maasailand from the coast to Lake Victoria.

Before he left in 1882, Thomson had met Henry Morton Stanley who had told him to take a thousand men – 'or write your will'. But the expedition was under-financed and the young Scotsman ended up with a full party of 143, all but a dozen of them described as the dregs and deadbeats of the Zanzibar waterfront. His adjutant, James Martin, was an illiterate sailor from Malta and about the only experienced member of the crew was Stanley's old headman, Muni Sera. Thomson's first foray, a careful probe inland of about 400 kilometres (250 miles), was aborted after the expedition's first encounter with the Maasai. In their full battle rig, he thought them 'splendid fellows'. But his caravan thought otherwise, reversed, and bolted back to the coast in just six days.

Thomson refitted, took on some more men, and managed to tack onto the back of an Arab caravan bound for the lake – but on the well-beaten track south of Kilimanjaro. He split just before the mountain, veered north, and soon ran into 'the arrogant savages who indeed look down upon all other tribes as inferior beings'.

His party was continually harassed by the inquisitive moran. 'They would frequently push me aside and swagger into the tent, bestowing their odoriferous, greasy, clay-clad persons on my bed or wherever best suited their ideas of comfort.'

But he was also impressed. They were 'magnificently modelled' and quite obviously a race apart in Africa. 'In their physique, manners, customs and religious beliefs, they are quite distinct from the true Negroes and the Galla and Somali,' he wrote.

At the expense of bales of trinkets, notably beads and vanity mirrors, Thomson was able to move forward without serious incident until the moran's curiosity in pinching and poking his white skin wore off. They then began to get more menacing.

'My goods were finished, and as I had no better stock in hand than a couple of artificial teeth and some Eno's Fruit Salts with which to keep up my reputation as the wizard of the north, my position was doubly dangerous.'

But Thomson's tricks of instant 'boiling' water, the vanishing teeth and sticks that sparked into flame were enough to get him going again – this time due north and into the comparative safety of the high-forested Satima Range which offered the additional comfort and reassurance of icy Scotch mists in the mornings. He named the mountains the Aberdares, after Lord Aberdare, the founder-president of the Royal Geographical Society.

Thomson went on to explore the great massif of snow-spiked Mount Kenya, crossed the Rift Valley, and reached Lake Victoria in December 1883. He spent the New Year shooting the local versions of stag and grouse on the Mount Elgon moors, then took a direct bearing on Mombasa for his line of retreat. He was gored by a buffalo on the way and very nearly died. And it was said to be soup made from diseased meat provided by his macabre friends, the Maasai, that kept him alive.

Merker, who followed him 20 years later, described the Maasai as 'entirely treacherous and ruthless'. They could not stand peace 'for more than a few months at a time', he wrote.

When the war parties did gather for a cattle raid or a battle, it was mandatory to consult the laibon, or more properly *ol-oiboni*, who is a master of religious ceremonies, chief policy-director and teller of the future. He would deliver oracles on the right way to proceed with the military exercise, whatever it was – but based less on clairvoyance than on an elaborate intelligence network which fed him information on the strength and disposition of the enemy. He would also give instructions to the moran commanders on ritual preparations, which were deliberately complex as an insurance against anything going wrong. The laibon would then blame the moran themselves for missing out some vital injunction.

Charms, amulets and other artefacts of the sorceror's art were supplied in abundance. One concoction, containing a paste of snakes' eggs, was said to make the scouts invisible as they spied out enemy country. Other potions and horticultural symbols were applied to clubs for throwing – by left-handed warriors – into the enemy lines to create terror and panic.

Battle was preceded by a meat-eating party, seasoned with herbal stimulants, which worked up the moran to a state of trance – resembling an epileptic fit – called *a-push*, 'the shakes'. In this condition, the moran may be lethally dangerous to himself, or others, and must normally be forcibly restrained.

After the feast, the warriors collected their weapons and a few head of cattle for food on the march. Their parents and girlfriends spilt milk and mead to appease the spirits and the moran set off in disciplined squads. They might cover as much as 80 kilometres (50 miles) a day, for days on end – although Merker was not greatly impressed.

'The training of the warriors consists only of marching,' he wrote. 'They carry nothing heavier than their weapons and both before and during their marches they use the nerve stimulants freely so their performance certainly does not surpass that of German infantry.'

The general discipline and strategy of the moran force did draw approval, especially their tactical deceits of spears sheathed in grass to prevent reflection and sandals worn back to front to confuse trackers.

In battle itself, the moran would either form defensive squares, like the Romans, or attack with classic manoeuvres using centre, outlier and reserve units.

Merker covered the Maasai military tradition in great detail and, like Thomson, stirred up great interest in the tribe in the universities of Europe. At that time, the most influential of all Maasai was a laibon called Mbatian. He had only one eye, but apparently saw the future with colourful precision. He foretold the imminent arrival of an 'iron rhino – with strangers of flamingo pink on its back'. And that was disaster, he said. 'I see the end for my children and the land. The strangers will come and kick my people down and keep them under their feet, like naughty children, although they may be brave moran and strong.'

Mbatian also predicted the onset of epidemics of smallpox and rinderpest, which would sweep down from the Horn of Africa and decimate both herds and people in the last decade of the 19th century. He died before it all happened – his power at least equal with that of the Abyssinian emperors, the last imperial chieftain in Maasai territory, which then extended over 207,000 square kilometres between the great lake and the coast, from Baringo in the north to Kongwa in southern Tanganyika.

Like Bismarck, his contemporary, he had hammered a union of the tribal factions, held power among them for ten years, and created the first fleeting 'nation of the Maasai'. When Mbatian died, it began to break up – first through in-fighting, then decimation by the twin plagues, and finally erosion of Maasailand at the agricultural fringe on the western highland of the Rift Valley. But it was a slow wearing away, like the sanding of coral cliffs by the tide.

The old man's first son, Sendeyo, should have succeeded to the laibon's black rod of office, but the story is that he was robbed by a younger brother named Lenana. It seems he stood on Mbatian's blind side in a darkened hut, received the rod and the dying man's confused investiture, then emerged as laibon by acclamation of the assembled council of elders. Sendeyo argued angrily but got nowhere and left for Tanganyika to start a civil war with the northern sections, which stayed loyal to Lenana.

Mbatian himself was given the equivalent of a state funeral. His body was carried up the side of Oldoinyio Orok – 'the black mountain' – facing Kilimanjaro, where it was buried in a shallow grave. A headstone was positioned so that the first shafts of dawn light fell across the site of the skull.

Thirteen years later, in 1890, the smallpox and rinderpest epidemics arrived in two waves from Somalia. They killed more than half the people and above 80 per cent of the Maasai cattle herd. Starvation reduced many of the 25,000 survivors to beggary and – worse – vulnerability to Bantu tribes getting their own back after years of subjugation. A few were traded as slaves and taken to the coast.

But the more serious assault on the Maasai, with lasting political effect, was a thin line of division drawn through the middle of their country in the colonial carve-up of East Africa. At a conference in Berlin to determine British and German 'spheres of influence', the European powers took a ruler from the eastern centre point of Lake Victoria to the village of Vanga on the coast, broke the line at the base contour of Kilimanjaro and squiggled round it to give the mountain to Kaiser Wilhelm. His aunt, the Empress Victoria, got the northern part with its own display of snow on the 'Mbatian' peak of Mount Kenya.

Later, a royal land commission was to make the comment that the Berlin border in 1894, 'cut the Maasai people in two with no more concern for the justice or convenience of their administration than the scythe has for a blade of grass'.

The separation of Maasai sections and age-set 'brothers' was to become ideological, with the moran technically cold warriors in other people's conflicts which, with studious indifference, they declined to join.

By 1895, the epidemics were over and what the Maasai called *ol-maitai*, roughly a ten-year cycle of disaster and fortune (usually good rains), was on the upswing. They restocked with cattle and women from reprisal raids on the Kikuyu of the eastern Rift highlands. Or it was the Kamba on the Machakos plateau south-east of a new railhead by a reserve watering point they called *enkare nairobi*, for 'cold water'. Mbatian's pink strangers, the keepers of the clanking, hissing rhino, corrupted the term to 'Nairobi'.

A demonstration that the moran were again a force to be reckoned with was then played out in the valley of Kedong, just north of Nairobi at the foot of the Rift escarpment. It started when louts from a mixed Kikuyu-Swahili caravan started harassing Maasai women in a homestead, *enkang*. They ran off when a platoon of moran showed up but were caught and butchered with *il alema* short swords. The Maasai then set about the main caravan and massacred the lot – in all, 456 Kikuyu and 96 Swahili.

A British civilian, Andrew 'Trader' Dick, was in the area and decided to exact instant retribution on behalf of the Crown. He grabbed some of the Maasai cattle, led his riflemen after them up the wall of the Rift, and walked straight into a Maasai ambush where he was speared to death.

In the official inquiry that followed, the Maasai were acquitted on the grounds that they had been unreasonably provoked. But the British kept Mr. Dick's requisitioned cattle as compensation.

The laibon Lenana was bemused by British justice but was generally loyal when it suited him. He set about unifying the northern sections of the Maasai, then made an opportunist strike on his brother Sendeyo's legions in Tanganyika. The British then made him paramount chief of the tribe, although no such rank existed in the Maasai system of democracy.

Lenana lived comfortably on his wits through much of the colonial period, deflecting the British pressure for change by frequent shows of friendship but little practical response. He would turn up at the Royal Nairobi Agricultural Show to judge cattle, flagging his allegiance in a British army great-coat. But he failed to produce moran recruits for the army or police, although a few Maasai served as runners for the Royal Mail with an overall performance close to Olympic standard.

One achieved a record of 792 kilometres (495 miles) in 20 days – from Mombasa to Eldama Ravine in the Rift Valley – with 13.6 kilos (30 pounds) of mail on his back.

But the runners were soon redundant when sisal gunny sacks replaced the cleft stick and the British 'Lunatic Line' – the Uganda Railway from Mombasa – reached its original terminus at Kisumu on Lake Victoria.

The railway also brought Sir Charles Eliot to Maasailand as the first imperial overlord of British East Africa. This refined, scholarly man was fascinated and appalled by the Maasai in almost equal measure, and often in the same sentence.

They were 'magnificent layabouts; superb to behold', but 'of no economic use whatsoever'. He described their dress and culture in fine detail, and the degree to which all this has changed in the following 80 years – virtually not at all – is an accurate measure of Maasai progress against what elsewhere in Kenya is otherwise an instant leap into the 20th century.

Eliot had recommended a policy of integrating the Maasai in the new pan-African society of East Africa and settling them as tenant farmers or labourers on the colonial estates. But it never happened. They have merely been pushed back by the despised 'diggers of the soil' – African and European – on the western Rift highlands of the Mau Range and elsewhere on borderland which is marginally arable.

Vast fields of wheat and barley now patch the Mau wetlands, the effect of which is to cut them off from fall-back grazing in periods of drought on the plains. If and when the Maasai are finally broken up, it will be because they will be confined – like the American Indians before them – on barren reservations which cannot support the traditional pastoral life style.

The highland reserve on the Laikipia shoulder of Mount Kenya has long gone. They had been robbed of the land by the early colonial government with what local historian G.R. Sandford saw as 'gentle coercion'. The British argument was that if they gave up the Laikipia estates to white ranchers, they could have a great southern reserve from Nairobi to the Tanganyika border 'in perpetuity – so long as the Maasai shall exist'.

The Maasai have kept this central heartland more or less intact – relatively free of civilising development – through the British reign and much of Jomo Kenyatta's first independent African republic of Kenya. But it can't last; or so it would seem.

The land has already been fragmented by government surveyors into group and individual holdings, which, one by one, are being taken over in sales or leases to outsiders.

As a whole, pastoral Maasailand is required, maybe in the medium term, to contribute to the national cash economy. And that means something more than revenue from tourists, drawn by the Maasai wilderness, the wildlife and the warrior in his red flag toga, signalling defiance within sight of a thrusting, ambitiously advanced Nairobi.

Every *eunoto* graduation of the moran is potentially the last; every *ol-maitai* cycle of disaster dips closer to the point of no return for the old tribal structure and way of life.

It was the beginning of the end when Thomson arrived in Maasailand almost a century ago. It still is.

Opposite: Doting grandparent weans youngster on a form of porridge.

Overleaf: Mothers of the moran, cleared of any blemish of social misbehaviour, are free to join the celebrations and festivals – singing the praises of their sons.

Below: Close to middle age, these Maasai women find time for relaxation now that the stress of child-bearing demands has eased. Maasai men measure their wealth and prestige by the numbers of their cattle – and their male heirs.

Opposite: Matriarchs of the moran perform a dance of tribute honouring the courage, daring and bravery of their sons.

Below: Young Maasai maiden, entito, with beaded ruff, pertly aware that she must groom herself to earn the admiration of the moran for whom for some years she and her companions will be playmates.

Below: High on a plateau in Tanzania's Maasailand, a young daughter milks the herd of her father, an elder.

Opposite: Young girl tends the family's flock of goats and sheep – until recently probably the only formal kind of education most Maasai youngsters would receive.

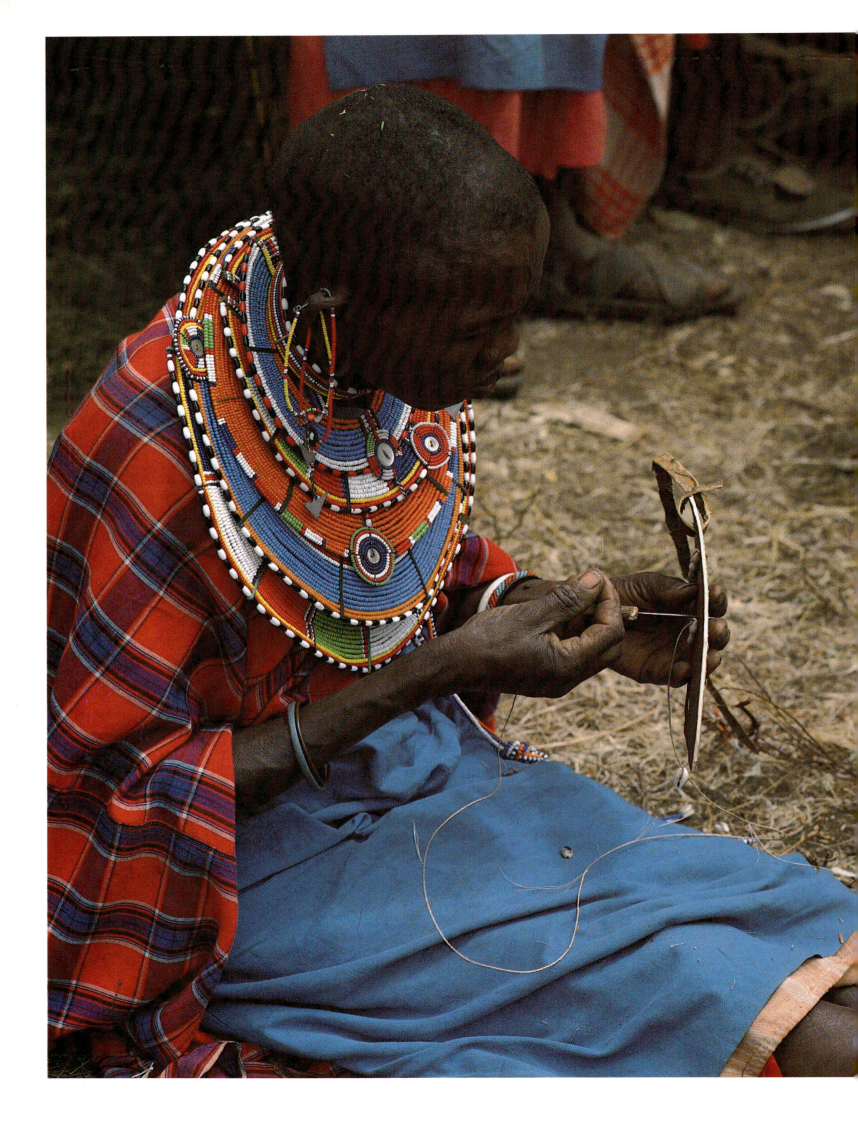

Opposite: Woman fashions sandals from home-cured rawhide. The needle and sinew used to stitch are hand produced too.

Overleaf: Elegantly decorated with ruffs and necklace, this ten-year-old girl is already wise about life among the moran in the manyatta where they live.

Below: Tough as old leather, moran feet nonetheless sometime stumble on a particularly vicious bed of acacia thorns. A bond brother lances the foot and removes the thorn.

2

WANDERERS

In this simple and clear age-grade system, a Maasai knows exactly where he stands in his local community and in the age-grade progression, as deference and respect for his age escalate automatically. The most elegant expression of this is in the changing forms of greeting between the generations. A baby is blessed by being spat on gently and anointed with milk mixed with earth which is marked on the infant's face very much like the sign of the cross. A youth bows and is touched lightly on the head by an elder in a gesture which Father Mol describes as 'love, blessing and protective feelings in one graceful movement'. Elders touch the forefingers of the right hand with those of equal dignity and respect.

These social relationships are obvious even to outsiders, whereas the clan-kinship bonds are totally obscure to everyone but a Maasai who knows precisely who he is in a complex system of blood-descent and geo-political groupings.

First of all, there is a division of all pastoral Maasai based on a genesis myth, with two equal 'families' or 'moieties' descending from the two wives of the founding father, called Maasinta. One woman built her hut on the right of the entrance to the village and had mainly 'red-brown oxen'; the other set up on the left and had a herd of 'black cows'. A Maasai is therefore said to be either 'of the right hand' or 'of the left hand'. But this distinction seems to be dying out now as is the descent myth itself, although Father Mol has found people in eastern Maasailand who refer to themselves as Il-Maasinta and retain the 'moieties' division.

The more important separation of one Maasai from another is by clan, sub-clan and kinship group, which is part of a tangled system by which the strength of the race is preserved. Basically, everyone must mix by marrying outside his clan, which means, in effect, that the relationship is never closer than third cousin. This exogamy law is absolute and is even built into the structure of the settlements where men are physically separated from their kindred women so that there can be no mistakes in courtships among young people of the same generations or age-grades. But, in any event, the subject of genealogy is thoroughly taught and in the same way he knows his cattle, a man will know precisely his own pedigree blood-line.

The difficulty of counting and analysing the kinship groups lies in the fact that the Maasai clans are as dispersed and thoroughly mixed up among the populations of Maasailand as are the clans in Scotland. They may once have had their separate fiefdoms, but these are now mostly

2

WANDERERS

An astute if unlikely analyst of the Maasai and the codes by which they live was the film actress, Shirley MacLaine, who wrote extensively about a visit to Maasailand in the 1960s.

'The more I travel, the more I realise that fear makes strangers of people who should be friends,' she wrote. 'But for a month in East Africa, I experienced what I felt was harmony, honour and complete trust of another people. They happened to be black people. They weren't civilised. They were primitive. And they were the most nearly fearless people I have ever known. Lying was beyond their comprehension and they believed in themselves. They were the Maasai whose independence is not only directed at the White Man but at the neighbouring tribesmen. And their justification for such independence is considerable.

'If they were afraid of the outside force applied to disrupt their "idyllic life", they suppressed it. Fear is despised. And perhaps that's what they sense in the White Man – fear! Perhaps that's what lies behind their refusal to accept any of the White Man's ways. Perhaps they recognise that fear breeds dishonour, cheating and lies, all of which are anathema to them. They may approve of the tangible results of "civilisation", but the methods by which they are obtained are contemptible.

'The sole ambition of the Maasai,' she thought, 'is no more than to herd the earth's cattle into their corrals. Their entire existence centres around their precious beasts.'

This much is accurate. In the Maasai system, at the closed centre of their society, wealth is still assessed in numbers of cattle, numbers of wives and children, and then in other livestock which are traded for cattle. Cash is inferior to the beads and cowrie shells which used to be the 'foreign exchange' for trade with the outside world – and about as significant in the pastoral economy. To the nomad, personal property is just an encumbrance.

Social distinction is partly what Shirley MacLaine said it was: fearlessness and physical courage. But it is also an exemplary life within the strict tribal ordinance of applied 'liberty, equality and fraternity'; of taking care of each other under a deeply religious creed ordained by the incomprehensible *Enkai*. Achievement is the right to wear a lion-mane head-dress at the moran's rite of passage, the *eunoto*, and power is respect and influence afterwards in the council of elders.

Their social welfare system, for instance, covers the sharing, or community ownership, of the walking wealth, land, housing, food, and

Previous page: Young girl with tiara smiles precociously. Early missionaries were appalled by the romantic attachments which sprang up – entirely normal for the Maasai so long as no pregnancy arises.

under a fairly permissive sexual code even each other. They are free to sleep where, when, and with whom they please so long as they confine themselves to their age-mates, obtain consent and avoid breaking a complicated set of rules guarding against in-breeding.

Their internal government is persuasive rather than coercive if judged by the ratio of the elders' talk under a fig tree to any consequent restrictions on individual freedom.

There is no printed paper in the Maasai administration of themselves; no notice boards and no kind of official communication more substantial than discussion. The old-fashioned political system of the Maasai is perhaps not far from what the 'new philosophers' of the sixties in Europe suggested for the next millenium now that God, Marx and mammon capitalism are 'dead' or 'discredited'.

Among other things, the 'new philosophers' advocated devolution of government to the village level; 'to small cells of people addressing themselves to issues that affect their individual lives', avoiding ideologies and monolithic central structures of government. It also rejected state or religious legislation in favour of a personal code of honour, integrity and generally decent behaviour. All this, roughly, is the basis for the traditional Maasai system of self-government.

Each section of the tribe has defined boundaries which, in principle, enclose enough lowland range and permanent water or high wetlands to support the nomadic wandering of people and stock in all seasons. But the administration of this balanced economy, as well as just about everything else in the life of a section, operates mainly at the level of the *enkutoto*, or locality. Each of these is made up of one or more moveable settlements which together amount to a self-contained social and economic unit, a loose commune of families which tend to get on with each other or otherwise move to a more congenial neighbourhood.

The families may be related, but generally not, because historically the separation of clan and kin has been found to reduce the chance of disputes over cattle and grazing, which technically belong to the tribe as a whole. However, when arbitration or community decisions are needed, the sole and absolute authority is a select group of age-set spokesmen in the location, meeting as the council of elders – the *enkiguena*.

Sometimes in consultation with retired or 'venerable' elders, they take all the major decisions, like moving the kraals to new pastures. They also sit in judgement on any individual infringement of the code of Maasai ethics and customary law, although in many cases they find that what may be a civil or criminal offence in other societies is reasonable free expression for the Maasai.

There is in fact a full body of oral law in four main sections covering sins against the tribal sections, crimes against individuals, small daily faults, and whatever is socially unbecoming a moran and a Maasai.

Usually the council-cum-court of elders deals with everything but the worst sins of treachery or cowardice in war, sacrilege, incest and witchcraft.

Formal execution or death by extreme cruelty such as burning or torture is unknown. And in no section of the Maasai penal code is the principle of 'an eye for an eye' applied. In almost every case, the outcome is 'horse-trading' – fines payable in cattle.

Blood revenge by the family of a murdered man – though not of a woman – is not permitted but when it does happen it is treated as a 'crime of passion'. But normally the convicted man or his family or clan settles the affair with the payment of damages in cattle. The deal may be done in formal proceedings with testimony presented occasionally by an official spokesman of the killer, or by elder counsellors chosen for their eloquence and knowledge of precedents.

A complaint may also be traded off, out of court, in a process called *amitu*, 'to make peace', or *arop*, which is a substantial apology and not a bribe as it is usually translated. The Maasai deny piously that there is any form of corruption in their society and that no-one would think of offering inducements to avoid prosecution or for any other socially unbecoming motive.

Another judicial process peculiar to the Maasai is the system in which old people with keen memories are consulted in difficult cases to provide reference for any precedent.

There are ceremonies for purification of all past sins and rituals in which a young animal is slaughtered in a sacrifice not unlike the old Hebrew 'cleansing of defilement' of a new-born child.

Father Frans Mol takes this image of the child as the start of a favourite metaphor he has for the life of a warrior, relating it to the course of 'the black river', Enkare Narok, which flows south-west off the western Mau escarpment of the Rift Valley and divides Kenya Maasailand almost exactly in half.

Its source is located somewhere in the dark Mau forest 3,000 metres (10,000 feet) above. It then emerges as a young stream, running and tumbling down rocks and deep-cut gorges to the Loita Plains where it broadens and becomes more impressive. From there on, it wanders through gallery woodlands of acacia 'tall and smooth-skinned as thighs of the warriors'. Then, finally, at about the halfway stage, it joins the sluggish 'brown river', Euaso Ng'iro, and begins a stately descent to almost casual evaporation in the desert north of Lake Natron in Tanzania.

In Father Mol's imagery, each section of this course corresponds to the character and status of a Maasai man in each of the distinct divisions, or age-grades, of his life.

In infancy, he is in a 'state of grace', in close communion with God, symbolised by a tuft of hair grown on the crown of his head.

Then, as soon as he can toddle, he is sent out with the calves and lambs; the cockade on his scalp is gone and his hair begins to grow.

At any time from 13 to 17, his 'boyhood', *ayiokisho*, is ended abruptly in a painful circumcision ritual at which he stays silent and brave while his parents writhe and scream for him in simulated agony.

After that, he becomes a warrior-recruit, proving his courage and endurance in long expeditions with his age-mates; in blooding his spear on young animals and birds and perhaps in provoking fights with the moran of other sections.

Eventually a company of these boys is allowed to set up a *manyatta* as junior warriors and, if the weather is good and there is plenty of help at home, free to spend the next two or three years doing anything or nothing as they please until serious responsibilities arrive after the graduation to senior warriors, at the *eunoto*.

The man is then at the centre of his society. He directs the stock and range management business of the community, takes part in defence, security and perhaps local government affairs, and is free, at the age of about 30, to retire from the moran and become a junior elder. When this happens, he moves out of the *manyatta* into a family enclosure, *enkang*, and, at an unspecified time, becomes a senior elder, usually via a meat eating ritual, called *ol ng'esher*.

From then on his prestige and influence increase until he eventually retires with the other members of his age-set. He might then be a consultant on all temporal and spiritual affairs as a 'venerable elder' until he dies and is left out in the bush for swift disposal by the elements and scavenging hyaenas. There is nothing more; no 'after-life' in eternal green fields among his ancestors. This is not part of the Maasai's religious imagery – or at least they 'don't know', or 'can't be sure'.

In this simple and clear age-grade system, a Maasai knows exactly where he stands in his local community and in the age-grade progression, as deference and respect for his age escalate automatically. The most elegant expression of this is in the changing forms of greeting between the generations. A baby is blessed by being spat on gently and anointed with milk mixed with earth which is marked on the infant's face very much like the sign of the cross. A youth bows and is touched lightly on the head by an elder in a gesture which Father Mol describes as 'love, blessing and protective feelings in one graceful movement'. Elders touch the forefingers of the right hand with those of equal dignity and respect.

These social relationships are obvious even to outsiders, whereas the clan-kinship bonds are totally obscure to everyone but a Maasai who knows precisely who he is in a complex system of blood-descent and geo-political groupings.

First of all, there is a division of all pastoral Maasai based on a genesis myth, with two equal 'families' or 'moieties' descending from the two wives of the founding father, called Maasinta. One woman built her hut on the right of the entrance to the village and had mainly 'red-brown oxen'; the other set up on the left and had a herd of 'black cows'. A Maasai is therefore said to be either 'of the right hand' or 'of the left hand'. But this distinction seems to be dying out now as is the descent myth itself, although Father Mol has found people in eastern Maasailand who refer to themselves as Il-Maasinta and retain the 'moieties' division.

The more important separation of one Maasai from another is by clan, sub-clan and kinship group, which is part of a tangled system by which the strength of the race is preserved. Basically, everyone must mix by marrying outside his clan, which means, in effect, that the relationship is never closer than third cousin. This exogamy law is absolute and is even built into the structure of the settlements where men are physically separated from their kindred women so that there can be no mistakes in courtships among young people of the same generations or age-grades. But, in any event, the subject of genealogy is thoroughly taught and in the same way he knows his cattle, a man will know precisely his own pedigree blood-line.

The difficulty of counting and analysing the kinship groups lies in the fact that the Maasai clans are as dispersed and thoroughly mixed up among the populations of Maasailand as are the clans in Scotland. They may once have had their separate fiefdoms, but these are now mostly

Overleaf: Two young girls, intoyie, *one newly attached to the manyatta and the moran, the other approaching the rite of passage – circumcision – which will ready her for marriage.*

guessed at, and the important territorial divisions of the Maasai are those of the 20 *il-oshon* – self-governing, sovereign independent units: the largest, Il-Kisonko, in Tanzania; the smallest, Il-Moitanik, in northern Maasailand.

There is always some form of loose federation among them; two or three *il-oshon* may consult the same laibon and are therefore spiritually united. But in effect each section goes its own way socially, and this separate development has resulted in considerable cultural divergence.

For instance, if one Maasai is shown a photograph of another, his first response would probably be: 'What group is he?', *ke olialo osho?* – although he might be able to tell himself from the distinctive designs of the bead-work, ornaments, overall dress and hair fashions. If the two were to meet, they might have difficulty in understanding each other.

But these are minor distinctions. Fundamental is the similarity in the way all Maasai live out their lives from one ceremony of transition to the next.

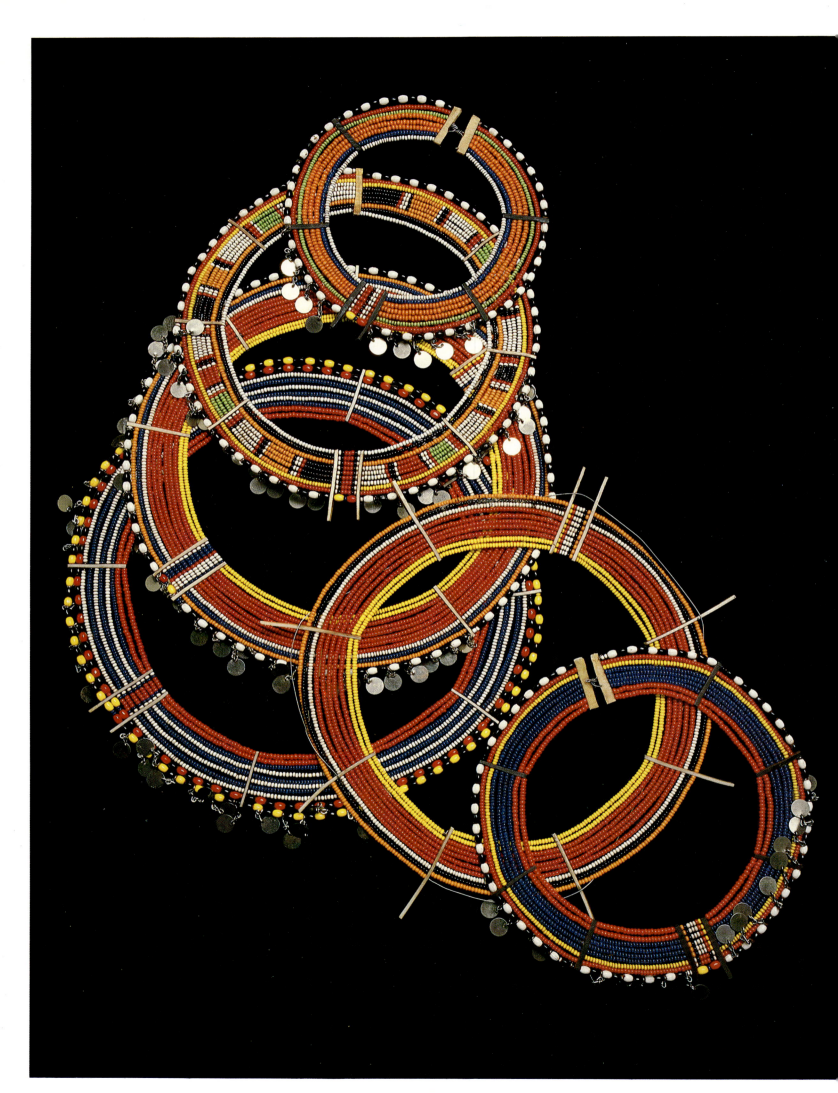

Below: Left – Beaded earrings called il tanga; *Top right – A woman's earrings from the Amboseli region; Centre – Married woman's earrings of beads and leather for the extended ear lobes; Bottom right – Delicate and unusual earrings.*

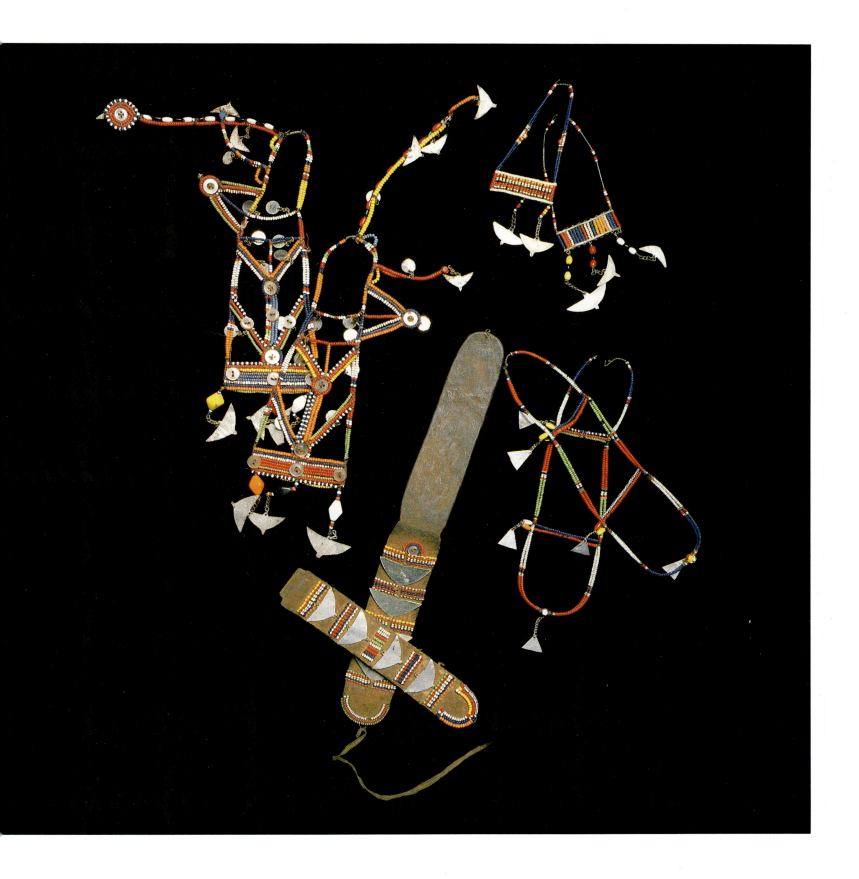

Below: Two pairs of woman's leather earrings. They must be worn before she goes out to milk in the morning.

Opposite: Colourful and long beaded ear ornament worn only by married Maasai woman with at least one circumcised son.

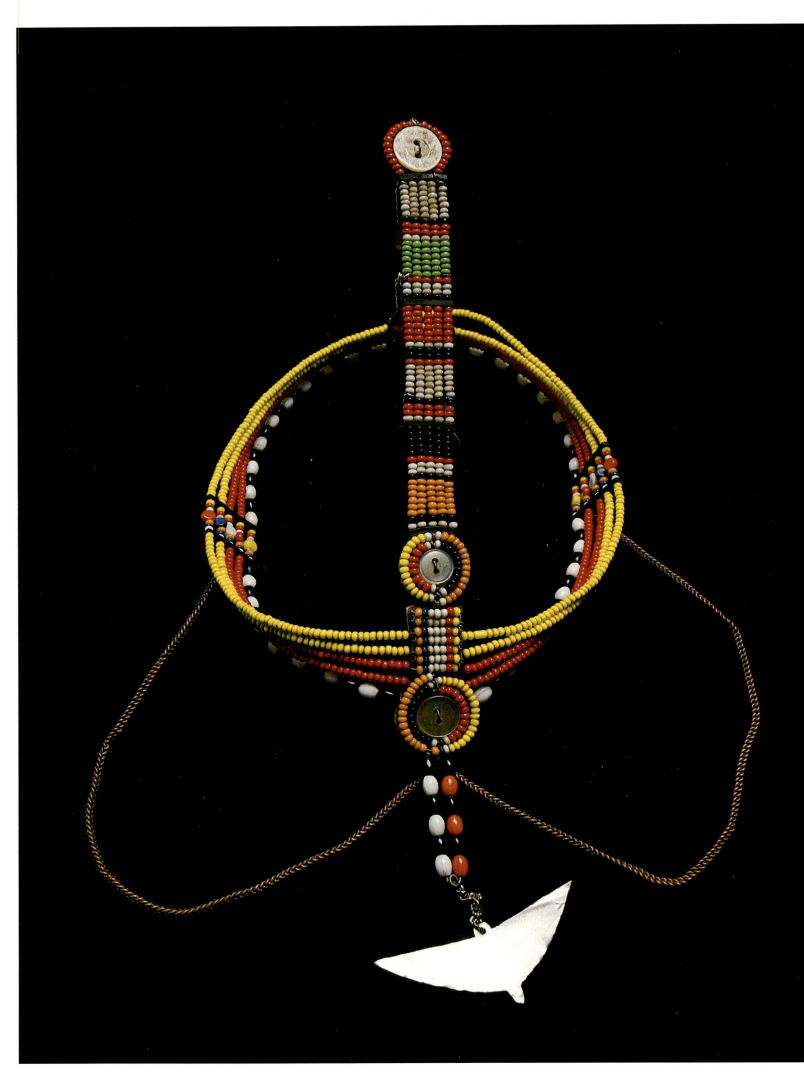

Opposite: '999' ornamental woman's headband named after the police cars with swirling lights on top.

Below: Typical Maasai head jewellery.

*Below: Centre – Warrior's pectoral ornament that
went out of fashion in the 1950s; Bottom right –
Necklace for men or women – maybe for good luck;
Left: Men's, women's and children's bangles.*

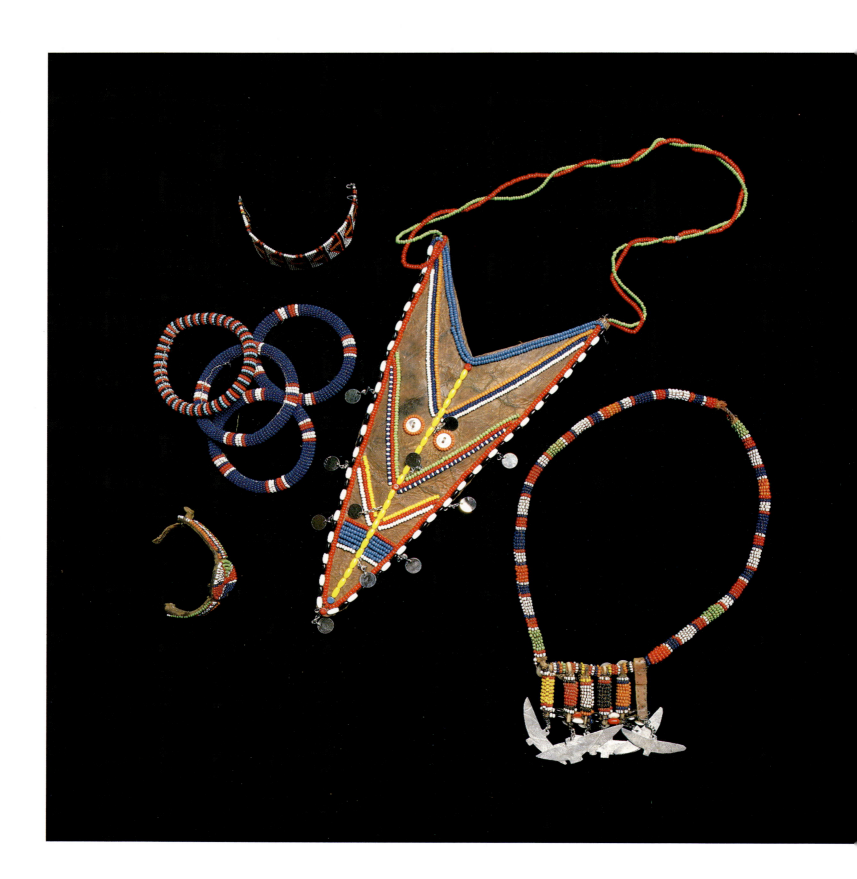

elow: Unmarried girl's leather belt.

Above: A wedding necklace, enkarewa, *and earrings*
el tanga.

Above: Moran with club, orinka, *and spear. Above right: Beaded scabbard for the Maasai short sword,* ol alem.

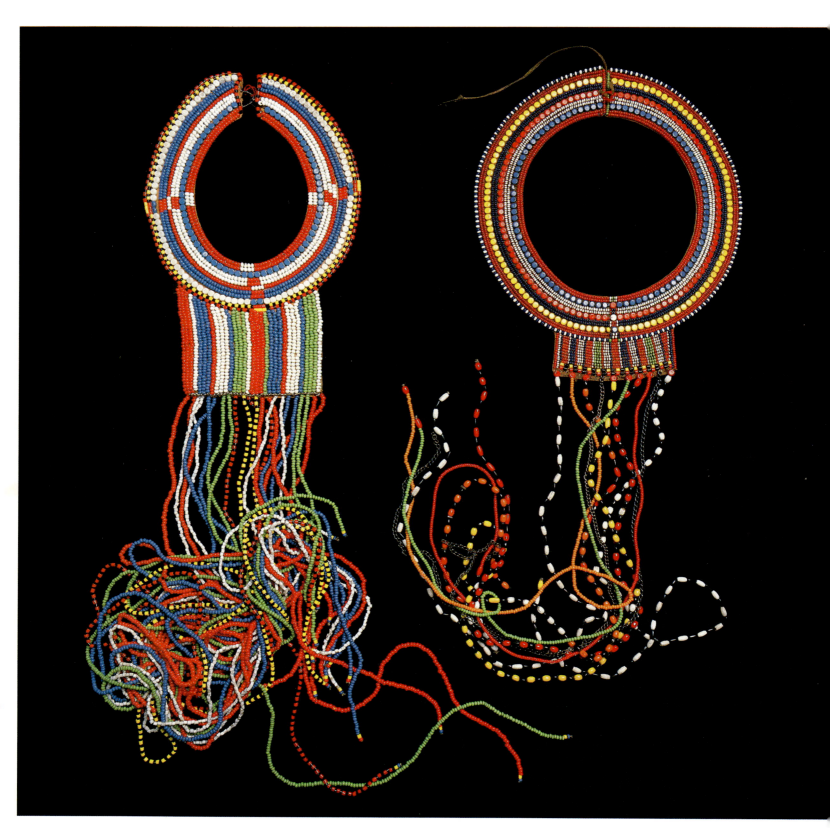

Above: **Enkarewa,** *special celebration necklaces with streamers.*

Opposite: Women with gourds filled during the daily milking.

Above: Gourds worked by carvers of the Kamba tribe.

Above: Traditional Maasai containers fashioned from milk gourds.

Below: Wooden cattle bells and those fashioned from the horn of the kudu.

Below: Collection of the powerful clubs, irinkan, used by Maasai warriors.

Overleaf: Moran elevated to status of junior elder.

3

INITIATION

Three main rites of passage are common to all sections of the Maasai, but the timing, form and ritual of the ceremonies vary considerably. Any description of these events is therefore relevant and accurate to only one group of people at a particular time and place.

The first of the rites is the circumcision of young boys which initiates a new generation or age-set of moran. Novelist Richard Llewellyn wrote a graphic account, but more interesting was the curtain-raiser he saw, which was anything but standard practice.

It started with the youngsters pestering their fathers and godfathers, *il pironito*, as soon as the laibon, in consultation with the elders, announced the opening of a 'circumcision season'. Although this involves the entire section, it's normally left to parents to make individual arrangements for their sons. In this case, the old men were not persuaded. They delayed for weeks until they considered the younger herd-boys were fully capable of taking over the stock from their elder brothers.

The initiates grew more and more impatient until they applied the ultimate pressure of a wild, Pamplona-style corrida, *omowuo olkiteng*, in which boys bring down a bull by the horns.

The day was chosen, the parents and elders gathered, and a large black bull was led into the arena inside the enclosure where, as the writer observed, the youngsters stood 'without linen, waiting'.

At the right moment of theatre, the counsellor of the senior moran raised and lowered his club of office and started a mad stampede of the boys, charging and yelling and fighting each other with the intention of grabbing the bull's boss and forcing it to its knees.

'Until then,' Llewellyn wrote, 'fighting had meant a skirmish with wooden spears and swords, or wrestling in the mud and dust and never more than a few scratches and bruises.' But in this melee, 'hands pulled, punched, tore; the bull bellowed and kicked…and the crush of bodies brought a blood craze'.

Eventually one of the boys managed to hold the bull's head still for a few seconds and it was all over. The counsellor blew a halt on a kudu horn and the fathers moved in to sort out their sons from a tangle of blood-and-dust-grimed bodies.

The point had been made and the elders were more or less obliged to get on with organising the ceremony. This would never be as dramatic as the bull fight, but it also entailed a public display of spirit and courage in an extremely painful metamorphosis from boy to junior moran.

According to another observer, circumcision is 'the central mystery of

Previous page: Girlfriends of the morans, spend months preparing for the eunoto *ceremony.*

Maasai society', but also 'a ritual designed to impress upon the boys that their rebirth as adults is of prime importance to themselves and the tribe'.

What happens is that the blood-bond between the boys and their parents is transferred to an age-set of brothers in circumcision. This permanent allegiance is sworn immediately after the initiation as moran and then at other rituals over a period of three to four years.

The laibon presides over the circumcision season, but always in consultation with the local elders. They work out how many moran are needed for the security of the section and induct about half the required number in a first or 'right-hand' circumcision age-group. They then declare a closed season for a few years until enough youngsters are old enough to be made moran in a second 'left-hand' recruitment, which is then held open until the full complement of the moran army is filled. The two age-groups amount to a complete age-set, which is eventually given a formal name and regarded as a corporate generation of the Maasai.

The challenge of the circumcision ritual may be judged from a close observation of one boy's initiation into the moran of the Loita section.

He appeared well before sunrise one day and stationed himself outside his mother's hut. The enclosure of about fifteen large family homesteads was quiet and the cattle were only just beginning to stir in the central compound. A fire flickered close to where the boy stood, but he still shivered in the chill of the morning, dressed in nothing but a black leather apron hung across the front of his body. By his side was a branch of the wild olive, one of four trees sacred in Maasai ritual and the insignia for circumcision.

After about an hour, the sky lightened and the enclosure came awake. People milled about in and out of the thorn-fence boundary, tended the cows and afterwards breakfasted, like the calves, on steaming milk. The celebrants then gathered outside the mother's hut and in due course she appeared in a gown of deep-tan leather decorated with a beaded head-band, earrings, wide necklace ruff, amulets, bracelets and coiled gaiters. Her finery and smiling chatter masked the nervousness she almost certainly felt. She was a widow and comparatively poor, so it was an important moment for her as her eldest son, the small boy in black beside her, was about to become a man and realise her hopes for prosperity.

After a while the surgeon arrived and sat a little apart from the group, applying the traditional white chalk paste in circles around the boy's eyes. He was an elderly man, probably a Dorobo from the nearby Nkuruman forest, but in any case clearly not a full Maasai. When he was ready, he signalled the boy's sponsor, who went inside the widow's hut and emerged with two other youngsters. They were also dressed in black aprons but wore head-dresses made of feathers and small stuffed birds which signified they had already been circumcised. They stood either side of their 'age-mate', solemn-faced, like acolytes at a high church service.

In response to a nod from the sponsor, they then walked the candidate across to the central compound of hard-packed cow-dung which shone in the low light of the sun like a polished dance floor. They stopped, turned to face east and began to sing, swaying rhythmically and beating time with sticks, which were also used to touch the candidate's cheek and lift his black drape to expose his genitals. The hymn was long, monotonous, plaintive and without melody.

When it was finally over, the three boys returned to the widow's hut, collected a large rawhide from the roof and went out of the enclosure through the candidate's family gate. They waited silently as the sponsor and two presiding elders robed themselves in ochred and beaded capes and led out a procession of the villagers to form a full arena theatre around the boys. An elder then unfastened the candidate's apron leaving him naked for anointment with cold water poured from a large earthenware pot. No one made a sound except the boy's mother who stood close by, wailing softly.

While this was going on, the cowhide was laid out between three olive branches, which was an altar table for the circumcision operation itself as soon as the baptism ritual was completed. The boy was dressed, but this time with the drape hung down his back leaving the front of his body exposed. He was led to the hide couch and seated gently in the middle of it, with one elder kneeling behind, pinning his arms, and the other two on either side, spreading his legs and holding them wide apart. The painted surgeon then approached holding a sharp knife, a flat, broad spatula of honed iron. He knelt directly in front of the boy, took hold of his foreskin, pulled it forward and sliced off the loose leading edge. Two incisions were then made along the length of the penis on either side and as the skin underneath fell away it was pared off leaving a lower flap intact. The surgeon swabbed with his free hand, examined the wound carefully, then squared off the flap and trimmed away rough edges of skin. He worked slowly and meticulously, stretching the operation almost to five minutes, during which the boy neither uttered a sound nor seemed to move a muscle, even involuntarily. He merely watched closely with a set expression while his mother and relatives yelled his agony for him, lamenting and screaming, until someone actually cried out: 'It is finished!'

The mother continued to weep, but with relief and satisfaction that her son had endured the operation with properly silent and stoic detachment. After that, the sponsor dragged the boy backwards through the gate and into the mother's hut. The crowd followed and eventually regrouped inside the compound for the last act of the ceremony.

This was an ordinary bleeding of a bullock, but ritualised by the two moran and a young girl specially chosen for the performance. They were robed in beaded capes and afterwards bowed their heads for a blessing by the newly circumcised boy's mother, who prayed over them and smeared butter on their scalps and foreheads. One of the moran then tied a strap round the steer's horn and reined it in firmly while the other slipped a second leather thong round its neck as a tourniquet to enlarge the jugular. He lifted a shallow-tipped arrow to a small bow, checked that the restraining slat of wood at the base of the tip was securely in place, and shot the arrow carefully into the vein. It was then removed and the girl caught the thin spout of blood in a gourd, filled it about three-quarters full and finally plugged the wound in the bullock's neck with a mixture of moist cattle dung and dirt. The blood was later stirred with a stick to remove the filaments, blended with milk and fed to the boy, now formally in convalescence, *osipolioi*.

Under normal circumstances, his father would begin immediately to arrange a feast, mainly to enjoy the reflected admiration and respect to which he would be entitled after his son's exemplary performance during the operation. He would light a ceremonial fire with juniper twigs, slaughter two or three unblemished black bullocks, and entertain lavishly for a day or two, with gallons of honey-beer assisting his narrative on the quality of his blood-line and his right to greater deference in meetings of elders.

If it had gone badly at the circumcision, the feast would have been short and the father abused as a no-good and a coward.

In this particular case, since there was no father, the boy's sponsor celebrated, accepted the plaudits, and spoiled his godson during his two-week seclusion in his mother's hut.

After their circumcision, the warrior cadets of the Maasai tend to go wild for a while, running about the countryside, shooting birds for their head-dresses, chasing young girls, annoying the junior elders, and generally making a nuisance of themselves.

Usually they set up a light camp in the forest, try nerve stimulants for the first time, and tell each other desperate stories from the Maasai equivalent of 'cowboys and Indians' folklore. In the old days, they were much more dangerous than they are now, with a tendency to try blooding their distinctive white spears on a passing caravan or in a raid on a Bantu village.

Once they had done this or otherwise 'distinguished' themselves, they could set about painting their shields with emblematic claims to warrior status. At that time, the shield markings were easily decipherable as an announcement of the owner's tribal section, special bravery, and age-grade. They started with black and grey sectional and group devices on a white background, designed by their sponsor or a respected warrior. If one of the boys happened to be recognised for a particular act of courage, he would be allowed to add a brightly coloured medallion.

At some stage, the newly circumcised conscripts, dressed in black clothes and wearing head-dresses of stuffed birds, would take a chance and mark their shields with a broad stripe of red paint made from laterite clay and the juice of a solanum plant. This was the coveted warrior's mark, and they would parade it outside a *manyatta*, taunting the junior elders with a vocal opinion that they were getting too old and feeble and should retire to make way for a braver, stronger generation. The effect might be to amuse the elders or so annoy them that they would attack the offenders' camp at night, thrash the youngsters, and make them scrub the red off their shields the following morning.

Eventually the youngsters got their way, but perhaps not until the laibon had announced the completion of an age-group at a ceremony during which, at one time, a bird is buried whole as a curse on anyone circumcised during the closed season without the laibon's express permission.

The setting up of a warriors' *manyatta* is also ritualised, but without imported witchcraft and strictly in the Maasai religious idiom, including the sacrificial slaughtering of cattle. The procedure varies. Sometimes a bullock is suffocated with the skirt of a married woman and blood drunk straight from a slit in the animal's throat. Sometimes, as at the *eunoto* ceremony, the new junior warriors are anointed with raw meat by selected elders and touched on the forehead with the heart and lungs which they bite and swallow.

An American professor, Dr. Alan Jacobs, described it in a 1971 report to the Kenya Government: 'During the first day of construction of the *manyatta*, ritual fire-making was again used to symbolise the unity of the village and the special relationship of its members to the alternate age-set above', he wrote. 'Once the site had been selected, twenty-eight pure white cows and one black bullock – colours which signify "joy" and "solemnity" respectively – were driven ahead of the warriors to the site to form the core of the village herd.

'A large white rock and bits of grass were placed ceremoniously in the centre of the village by the "firestick" elders *il pironi* (two generations senior to the graduates) who then called upon God to bless and protect their sons and to cause their herds to increase "like the white rocks and grass which cover the earth".

'As mothers were assigned to places at the circumference of the village to build their warrior sons' houses, the black bullock was caught, thrown and held to the ground while ritual fire was kindled on his left side by the elders. The kindling was then used to ignite a bonfire of special woods placed over the buried rock and bits of grass. As it burned during the night, each warrior gave a burning ember to his mother to light her household hearth.'

This hearth fire would be safeguarded and revered like a European or American eternal flame for dead heroes. In Maasai ritual, fire is the most potent symbol of life. At any time, a hut would be considered 'dead' if it were not warmed by fire; but on this occasion the fire was 'holy' and a mother would sin gravely if she allowed the token of her son's new life in his first *manyatta* to flicker out and die.

In a sense, the *manyatta* itself is a symbol for some of the more important aspects of the prescribed life for junior warriors. Their first duty is to protect the community from predators, animal or human; their fitness for this is indicated by the absence of a perimeter barricade of thorn bush. They have to learn Maasai genealogy, for which purpose the *manyatta* is split in half, one for each moiety, and the huts sometimes arranged in a sequence by clan and family.

The moran are supposed to live absolutely as one body of brothers. No one is allowed to drift away and sleep or eat alone, or even relieve himself except in company with one or more of his age-mates. In the structure of the *manyatta*, this bonding is represented by a close grouping of the huts, each of which is a large barrack-room for a full band of moran, plus their mothers and girlfriends. They neither own cattle nor undertake regular stock duties, so there are none of the interior kraals that clutter an enclosure of married families.

The compound of a *manyatta* is a wide-open leisure space for walking about, talking and dancing, which, with courtship, are nowadays said to be the main diversions of the warriors. The fact is that they are bored now that they are forbidden to stage a lion hunt – although they still do occasionally. These days it would be a furtive affair, certainly nothing like the performance they put on in the 1930s for Edward, Prince of Wales.

The colonial governor of the day, Sir Edward Grigg, described the event in his book *Kenya's Opportunity*, which he said 'showed the amazing personal bravery of the Maasai warriors. Their method is to locate the lion, surrounding him only with their painted leather shields and broad-hafted spears. As the ring closes and spears are cast at very short range, the lion invariably charges and the warrior who receives the charge is always mauled.

'This particular lion hunt followed tradition, though its tension was curiously enhanced by a flight of aeroplanes containing (I think) newspaper men, which circled overhead. One magnificent black-maned lion was duly surrounded and speared, then two unrehearsed incidents livened the day which was very hot and still.

'The Prince of Wales and my wife were watching the hunt unarmed when a second black-maned lion leapt out of a thicket and confronted them at very close range. The Maasai, however, turned at once and surrounded him; another warrior was mauled but the lion was killed in the same way.

'I was standing about a hundred yards behind with a double-barrelled rifle, having Lord Delamere, Baroness Blixen and some other ladies under my care. This duty I was discharging as a dignified sinecure, when a third lion leapt out of a thicket half way between the Prince and our group.

'He turned his back disrespectfully upon the Prince and faced me, looking beetle-browed and indignantly lashing his tail. I was afraid of wounding him without killing him if I fired, so I decided to leave the initiative to him. The suspense seemed very long; but at last he tossed his head and loped away. The Maasai, having the Prince between them and him, had to let him go. For my part, I took off my hat to his departing hindquarters.'

Errol Trzebinski, a more recent historian, is a little more colourful in describing the event. There were about fifty moran engaged to entertain the Prince, Trzebinski wrote, all 'elaborately finger-painted with red-ochre which dries and contrasts strangely, like a bleached tattoo on their shiny ebony skins in dulled earthen squiggles and stripes.

'There is a great dignity and power in their bearing though they look as natural as cave-paintings – their bodies loose-limbed and at liberty to lunge and quiver.

'Armed with *rungus* clubs, shields and spears, the privileged in previous combat with lions are crowned with their victim's tawny mane, symbolising prowess. The lithe young men tremble. The excitement mounts in frenzy as they close in on the cornered lion.

'They begin to shout "*Simba* lion, *Simba, Simba*" until in a crescendo of noise and splintered yells the final thrusts are made in the recoiled body of the terrified cat.

'He dies from a menacing passion – of a type that is seldom witnessed or legally practised.'

For this reason, according to a present-day warrior, the young men are now obliged to apply their virility more frequently on their girlfriends. He was smiling as he said it, but around a *manyatta* of the Il-Kaputiei section there was clear evidence of close and even romantic association between the tall muscular moran in their late teens and early twenties and the flat-chested, narrow-hipped girls aged from about nine to 16.

Couples stood in the shade of the huts, talking intently with an occasional long, loose arm of a warrior draped across the shoulders of his girl. A few others were chasing about playfully and one girl was caught, hoisted high in the air, and lowered slowly, her expression changing from amusement to something more intense as she slid down the front of her warrior's body.

Later, at an important dance, the movements looked more explicit although the moran swear innocence of sexual intent. A dozen or more of the men formed a ragged line and began a rhythmic chant that sounded like...*Ooooooh-yah...Oooooo-yah*...a monotonous lion's growl and stacatto cough together with the thrust and withdrawal of their lower bodies. The girls positioned themselves directly in front of the men, made the same pelvic lunges and sang a high dying fall of...*Oiiiiii-yo... Oiiiiii-yo*...in a counterpoint chant. The bodies never actually touched, but it was always close.

For some reason, the men looked more fazed by the process than their partners – their eyes closed and sweat beading their foreheads, whereas the girls were smiling, bright-eyed and only biting their lips against the heavy slaps of their necklace ruffs.

After a while, a warrior broke out and started the second part of the dance. This consisted of two or three phenomenally high standing jumps, with head and chin thrust out and the body as dead vertical and rigid as the stick clamped in his right hand. Then, one after another, all the moran sprang up and down like red pistons, and usually finished off by moving forward, saying something to the girls and receiving a crescendo of *Oiiiiii-yo*…in response.

There are no orgies with the girls, rarely full intercourse, but plenty of play to the level of heavy petting. Sometimes a warrior will develop a special fondness for a very young girl, but for full sexual satisfaction he will either turn to a more mature girl in the *manyatta* or sneak off for a furtive affair either with the circumcised sister of an age-mate or a married woman. It happens more these days than it used to, but both activities are officially illegal and not undertaken lightly.

For instance, it would be a disgrace as well as an inconvenience for a warrior to get an uncircumcised girl pregnant, and he would have to make a public exhibition of any adultery at his *eunoto* graduation ceremony. The married woman involved would also have to admit her sin at this time if she happened to be a classificatory mother of a graduating moran.

Women are not obliged to be especially chaste, at least not by western definitions. They can sleep with whom they like so long as they keep within the laws of clan-kin relationships and confine their affairs to age-mates of their husbands. This is a fundamental tradition, although the practice is not always as matter-of-fact as the ethnologists imply.

The Maasai are polygamous by necessity: an ancient, practical response to a high infant and warrior mortality rate. To an extent they are also polyandrous, probably for the same reason, but also because of the 'one-body' concept of the age-group. In effect, a woman marries not one husband, but the entire generation of his brothers in circumcision. It is expected that a man will give up his bed to an age-mate guest. The guest will plant his spear outside the hut with a reasonable hope that he will be 'accommodated' for the night as announced. But the option is strictly with the woman. There is no coercion, no obligation, and only if she likes the look of the man will she, as she puts it, 'cross the hearth' to his bed.

The physical outcome, if there is any, would be without question the husband's child and his descendant in the patrilineal order of Maasai society. If there is any jealousy, age-mates dare not make it public.

Sexual mores among the Maasai are liberal. No one needs to be deprived; there are no sexless spinsters, no lonely old men and very few neurotic 'deviants'. In fact, the Maasai tend to be comparatively uncomplicated in the performance of the act.

Intercourse is entirely natural and as inconsequential and brief as a refreshment break for a half-gourd of milk. The Maasai usually kiss only relatives and they are unlikely to make much of a demonstration before or after intercourse. But this implies that they are incapable of 'romantic love' and 'tender attachment' and ignores the fact that a warrior might elope with his girlfriend or deliberately get an eligible woman pregnant so that she will be married to him rather than her family's candidate. A married man might conceivably confine himself to a cherished wife; a married woman could well leave home for a lover among her husband's age-mates.

A kind of divorce, *kitala*, meaning 'refuge', back in the wife's father's home is possible, usually for gross mistreatment of the wife. The proceedings are merely a matter of settling the details of a mutual agreement, with the husband retaining the children or recouping the original bride-price, plus substantial interest in livestock.

In many ways, their emotional response to each other is not exceptional. Above everything else, a man wants his woman to be a good mother and home-maker but he also appreciates a bright personality, a happy disposition and good looks.

The moran is often remarkable. So much so, in fact, that there have been a number of scientific expeditions in Maasailand to discover the extent and cause of the physiological differences between the Maasai and everyone else.

Two American scientists and a local 'Flying Doctor' who tested the stamina of fifty-three moran on a treadmill reported that their performance was of 'Olympic standard'. They also applied electro-cardiograph tests to 400 Maasai and found no evidence whatsoever of heart disease, abnormalities or malfunction. Moreover, in analysis of carbon-14 tracer checks, it was evident that despite an extremely high diet intake of animal fats, the Maasai system was able to suppress the cholesterol build-up to about 50 per cent of the level in an average American body. This immunity to heart problems was ascribed to the amazing fitness of the moran.

They are still in comparatively better condition than most other people, even without the excuse or opportunity these days for fast, long-range wars and cattle raids. Warriors spend most of their time now on walkabouts throughout Maasailand, beyond the confines of their sectional boundaries. They are also much more involved in cattle trading

than they used to be, since they develop and improve the basic stock by buying or bartering rather than stealing it as in the past.

A great deal has been written about the overwhelming preoccupation of the Maasai with cattle, but perhaps one story illustrates the point sufficiently. In 1945, Major Hugh M. Grant, a British livestock officer in Narok District, wrote in his annual report that he found it increasingly difficult to buy young beef from the Maasai. The following year he went about the Loita area requisitioning stock until he ran into the forceful objection of a warrior. The young man refused to part with a white bullock and offered ten other steers in lieu.

When this was refused, he committed what he almost certainly knew was the capital offence of running the Englishman through the heart with his spear. The elders tried to explain that the moran had acted reasonably 'under circumstances of extreme provocation' and could not be indicted under customary law. The white bullock had been bred and reserved for a ceremonial occasion and, in this case, was earmarked for slaughter at the warrior's *eunoto*.

But the moran was hanged.

Below: Moran fires an arrow into an ox's jugular. The spurting blood gushes into a gourd. Later, mixed with milk, it becomes a protein-rich 'Maasai cocktail' – a ritual drink for special celebrations and for the sick who need nourishment.

Opposite: Filaments removed after thorough stirring the blood and milk cocktail makes a nourishing meal for a senior elder.

Opposite: Two moran entertain themselves with bao, complicated play with pebbles moved up and down two lines of egg-shaped hollows in wood, here simulated by being scooped out of the sand of a dry river bed.

Below: New recruit to the ranks of the moran poses in the manyatta. His hair, shaven for his time in the cadet group, 'the shaven ones', il-aibartak, now begins to grow again to form the elegant and individual coiffure of the warrior.

Below: Childhood is mostly playtime for Maasai youngsters with sticks serving as make-believe spears although there is some teaching – mainly on warrior traditions and cattle keeping – from an appointed godfather, ol-piron.

elow: Childhood places more responsibility on girls
an boys. These three rest between their chores of
ilking and cooking in the village of the parents,
nkang.

posite: Wooden plugs in her ear lobes, beaded cklace, hair cropped tight and fetching smile, an tito tends the family goats.

Overleaf: Maasai houses reflect the community's nomadic life style: simple but sound. The low, wicker framework of thorn branches is swiftly daubed with mud and cattle dung and left to bake dry in the sun to provide effective shelter from both sun and rain.

low: Young herd-boy tends Maasai cattle on which community's entire culture is rooted – in legends, tory, lore and even language. In Maa, there are at st 30 words to describe the shape and hue of cattle.

4

MANHOOD

The 'coming of age', the *eunoto* of the warrior, is well known to outsiders and well documented. It is the most sustained and theatrical of the Maasai's religious and social observances, a grand pageant, with ten or more days of music, dancing and ritual. But although there has been plenty of graphic and accurate observation, there has been little explanation and interpretation of the ceremony.

However, one 'coming-of-age' performed by the Il-Oodokilani section in 1968 was described in the Maa language and is probably as close to the heart of the ceremony and as reliable an explanation as it is possible to get. The reporters were Benjamin ole Maora, a son of the divisional leader of the moran, and Konana ole Mulei, an Il-Purko section elder who provided comparative notes.

The event was announced as usual by the laibon after long and beery consultation with the elders. Runners were sent out to spread the word throughout the territory and after a few days, the first companies of warriors began to arrive. They came in single file, in full regalia, flying painted banners of leather, and danced with the excited host community of young girls in a non-stop reception festival that lasted about a week.

Then, when more or less the entire age-set was assembled, the laibon communicated with God and relayed divine approval for the start of the *eunoto*. It would begin at dawn the following morning.

First the warriors of the Il-Oodokilani – 'the-men-of-the-red-clothes' – painted their faces with chalk paste and staged a 'white' dance, which went on for two or three hours as a kind of march-past and tattoo.

When it was over, the men themselves became spectators at a suspense drama played by their mothers. One by one the women split up into those who were pure and those who had sinned by sleeping on the sly with the moran. These became despised Magdalenes who were not only in disgrace with their sons and cuckolded husbands but shunned and chased away from the ceremonies by the rest of the community. It was obvious that a few husbands had been unaware, until then, of their wives' misbehaviour, and there were some noisy domestic scenes on the sidelines! From then on these women, called *nkirikeny*, were banned, first from performing the song of celebration and then from constructing a holy circle of huts outside the village.

In the late afternoon, the moran regrouped for a second ensemble performance in the main arena. Some wore lion-mane or ostrich-feather head-dresses; all were freshly ochred and armed, draped in colobus monkey skins, and jangling with thigh bells and iron ornaments. They formed two lines facing each other and danced backwards and forwards singing songs, chanting tonelessly like a vesper chorus of monks until the sun began to set. They then laid aside their spears, swords and clubs in a ritual 'farewell to arms' and afterwards carried only the long wooden staffs of cattlemen and shepherds, symbolising their ownership, after the *eunoto*, of their first herds of cattle.

A select group was then detached from the rest by the *il piron* elders

Previous page: Horn of the greater kudu forms a wind instrument on which the summons for the moran to gather for the eunoto *ceremony is blown.*

who blessed them, gave them charms and sent them off for the night on special assignments. Seventeen of them were delegated to collect the white make-up from a far-off river bed; four to make ropes from the bark of the sacred rain tree; and four to gather sheaves of grass, the insignia of peace.

At the same time, the three outstanding warrior cadets were selected as permanent senior officers of the age-group. Two were spokesmen, one for secular and one for religious affairs; and the third as their deputy whose first duty was to produce a pure black bullock for a ritual sacrifice. This animal was force-fed through the night with milk, mead and potions provided by the laibon. Then at dawn, after the singing of the celebration hymn, it was laid on its left side by leaders of the left-hand circumcision group of warriors and smothered to death with the skirt of a married woman.

It died 'satisfactorily' for the graduating juniors, without making a sound or violent movement, which would have signified an unsettled future for them as the new senior defenders of the tribe. And since the slaughter had gone well, the moran celebrated with a dance, after which the arena was cleared of spectators for a secret communion ceremony. In this solemn ritual, the head of the dead animal was raised, a slit cut in its dewlap and the blood mixed with milk. A venerable elder then supervised the communicants, each of whom took a token sip direct from the dewlap and was individually blessed.

After this, the carcass was butchered and strung across a barbecue fire on eight forked stakes; the moran relaxed while it roasted. The band of holy mothers moved in to build an enclosure of hides around them and make a start on the 'inner sanctum' or physical heart of the *eunoto* – a special ceremonial building called the *osinkira*. They constructed a wicker frame, then stopped work while a contingent of warriors went off to collect heavier wood for the roof.

When the moran returned, a crowd of elders, women and children went out to greet them with hymn singing and then filed past on their right side, gesturing or pronouncing a blessing as they went. At the end of this long ritual, the laibon arrived and selected from the piles of wood three stakes, one of which was forked. These were carried into the *osinkira*, set up reverently with the cross-piece in between the two straighter poles and set in a hole in the ground. The scene was prayed over and sanctified by the laibon and became, in effect, the main altar setting for the *eunoto*.

By that time, the black ox that had been sacrificed was cooked and ready for distribution to the mothers and elders who took their share and left the enclosure so that a second secret ritual could be performed – the blessing of an honour guard of forty-nine warriors. These sat in a circle as an elder took round the brisket from the roast meat, anointed each moran in turn with the juices and offered it to him to bite.

A second elder blessed the warriors individually, a third took round a gourd of milk, and a fourth gave them honey-beer, which until that moment they had not been allowed to drink.

When this was over, they joined the rest of the moran in informal dances with the girls until late in the afternoon when the day's events concluded with a final consecration. A rein of cowhide, knotted for each clan, was woven into the framework of the *osinkira* hut. The same was done with the ropes of rain tree bark, the sheaves of grass were attached and a prayer was uttered to God to bless this 'new house of the moran'. After that, the holy mothers completed the roof and plastered the walls with cow dung so that a favoured group of elders could retire inside for a meal, beer and weighty discussion. The rest of the people dispersed to their own homes and the warriors to meat feasts in the forest.

Early the following morning, the men returned to the ceremonial building, sang a new hymn and then slaughtered a second black bullock. They roasted it, and when it was ready, sent cuts of meat to the mothers. The hide was also sent and this was pegged out by the women in an important but now obscure ritual, each mother hammering a peg for each of her warrior sons. Any adultress who dared to approach was driven off.

The moran danced for most of the afternoon and at sundown retired to the forest to perform a special dance before the slaughter of the last ox, donated by the moran's *oloburu enkeene*. This slaying signalled the beginning of the end of the *eunoto*.

The laibon stayed the night with the warriors and the following morning marked their foreheads and left shoulders with white paste before leading a procession into the charged atmosphere of the *manyatta* for the closing ceremonies.

These were unremarkable for most of the day, as much sensation as spectacle according to one witness: 'a Maasai kaleidoscope of changing and combining odours of dry grass, camphor bush, cattle dung, sour milk and wood smoke'. The strong earth colours and stark white decoration of the moran faded in sepia dust clouds kicked up by their fat-shined, dancing, stomping bodies. Then both performers and onlookers broke up and sprawled about in small groups.

This ragged pattern of carnival and solemn occasion spread across the day until late afternoon and an abrupt change of mood when the moran assembled for the ultimate trial in the life of the male Maasai: the climactic ritual of the *osinkira*.

The moran were all agitated. One or two of them threw a fit of the 'shakes'. They stood in line waiting for the laibon and the *ol piron* elders, sitting outside the hut, to pass judgement on each of them in turn. Those who had more or less observed the laws and honour code were allowed to enter the hut and urinate into a hole at the altar of stakes. The rest, for sleeping with uncircumcised girls or some other offence, were turned away to face the noisy scorn of the crowd and the wrath of their fathers – whose status in the community would from then on be reduced. After this final public event, the *eunoto* petered out in a few days of private celebration feasts and head-shaving wakes. Even the women excluded from the ceremonies since the first day were allowed to take part in the feasts – on payment of a collective fine of heifers! They and the rest of the mothers carried out the barbering at random, sitting their sons cross-legged on their circumcision hides – preserved especially for the occasion – lathering their heads with milk and shaving them carefully with razor blades. A balm of red ochre was then applied which soothed the irritation of the scalping, though not the warrior's grief at losing the full-grown, full-sculptured coiffure of a warrior.

From then on, the moran would probably stay on in the *manyatta* for a while with his gang of age-mates. Later when he felt ready for it, he would leave the *manyatta* and move into his parents' enclosure to be given an inaugural herd of cattle by his father and sub-clan. Although he then would be technically a junior elder, the warrior would not be confirmed in rank until after another 'rite of passage'.

In some cases, this is a private family affair, but the Il-Kisonko in Tanzania still make it a major festival of the full tribal division. It happens perhaps once every fifteen years, most recently over four days of a full moon at a holy place called 'the hill of the elders'. The site is said to have been used by the Il-Kisonko for the same ceremony for generations.

In many ways, the rituals are similar to the *eunoto*, involving the construction of an *osinkira* ceremonial hut, the slaughter of cattle, the drinking of ox blood, and the lighting of initiation fires with a doum palm stick and a hollowed board lined with dry grass.

The culmination of the rite is a blessing by the young elders' surviving sponsors outside the *osinkira*, with the initiates sitting facing the sunrise over the snowy skull-cap of Mount Kilimanjaro. The new age-set of elders is named and the festival ends with a jubilant banquet of beef and beer.

There is one final, autumn rite of passage for the men of the Maasai, which has been celebrated on a sectional basis by the Il-Loita, Il-Keekonyokie and Il-Purko sections in Kenya. It is called *enkang ool orikan* for the four-legged stool which the elders bring along with them to symbolise relaxation of the responsibilities of senior elders.

The last rites for the dying are virtually without ceremony. Like Father Mol's 'black river of Maasailand', life ends insignificantly and in all cases the body is left out for the scavengers. To bury the dead is considered dishonourable.

There are no requiems and no elegies for a dead Maasai. Highly respected male elders and senior women – those who live to a great age only – are given burial in cairns or piles of stones that allow Maasai to inter and commemorate honoured dead without having to dig in the earth.

Below: The girlfriends of the moran, intoyie, spend months preparing their part in eunoto – which is mainly to parade themselves in their most spectacular costumes with a centrepiece of a huge and heavy necklet ruff of beads.

Overleaf: Crowds gather early in the morning in the main settlement, enkang, awaiting the arrival of the moran after the warriors' night vigil. Clansmen and women from all over Maasailand gather for the occasion, some travelling hundreds of kilometres.

Preceding pages: Removed from the main settlement, moran gather under an acacia tree for one of the rituals of the eunoto, *presided over by a laibon and senior elders.*

Below: Moran in lion-mane and ostrich-feather head-dresses, which denote their elite status, are privileged observers of the rituals in the consecrated shrine, osinkira.

Opposite: Leadership of a moran company, esirit, *is awarded to the man honoured by both warriors and patrons,* il-pironi. *The criteria for the appointment of captain,* ol-aiguenani, *include qualities of courag and intellect.*

Left: Moran leaders await the summons to move in procession to the 'holy' house, osinkira, *where the laibon will perform the main rituals of the* eunoto.

Overleaf: Soon after dawn on the day of the eunoto, *the moran prepare the traditional white body decoration with chalk paste from a river bed.*

Preceding pages: Hyped up on herbal stimulants, the moran jog in single file to the main village, enkang. *It is a moment of great excitement – before the adulation of the crowd – and also some apprehension: their individual merits will be judged by a court of elders.*

Below: In full dress regalia and line abreast, warrior simulate an advance charge. In old days, just the sight of them was enough to start a rout among the enemy.

Below: Formation of marching moran approaches the village.

Overleaf: Moran and their girlfriends come to participate in the eunoto *ceremonies. The first two in line are among the 49 chosen to be shaved before the rest.*

Opposite: High-spirited moran in full body paint,
nturoto, waits for the **eunoto** parade to begin.

Below: Select leader of an elite squad of moran leads
his platoon forward for the rituals within the holy
house.

Overleaf: Two moran and their mothers on the eve of
the **eunoto** which will rank them all – the boys for
their behaviour as warriors, the mothers by the
prestige accorded their sons.

Below: Spectacular standing jump of the moran,
adumu, *which serves as competition and expression of masculinity.*

Below: Spindly, long-legged warriors move in and out of the encircling ranks as their turn falls to perform the leaping dance, adumu.

Below: An elder discusses the forthcoming judgement the **eunoto** *council of elders will deliver on his warrior son which, to some extent, will also determine the father's social status in the tribe.*

Below: Rigid moran, arms extended, is carried away until the trance passes. Instances of moran running amok with a short sword, ol alem, *or spear when in this state are not uncommon.*

elow: Coming round from the trance, a-push, *dicated by foaming at the mouth, a moran is helped* *walk away. Apart from the tension induced by the* *noto, the trance can also be brought on by drugs* *iled from roots and tree bark which the warriors* *rink on the eve of their initiation. In the past, these* *imulants were also taken on the eve of battle, the* *aasai equivalent of Dutch courage.*

Overleaf: Spray of milk from the mouth of an elder settles a benediction over squatting ranks of the eunoto *graduates.*

Right: Graduates from the eunoto *after their elevation to junior elders.*

Below: Shaven-haired moran near the end of the eunoto *ceremonies.*

Below: Moran applies white make-up for the eunoto ceremony. Patterns and application are spontaneous. Part of the moran arsenal is a short sword, ol alem, *not unlike those used by the ancient Roman legions.*

Opposite: Chalk paste, enturoto, *provided for t̶ moran to paint their bodies with traditional decorations.*

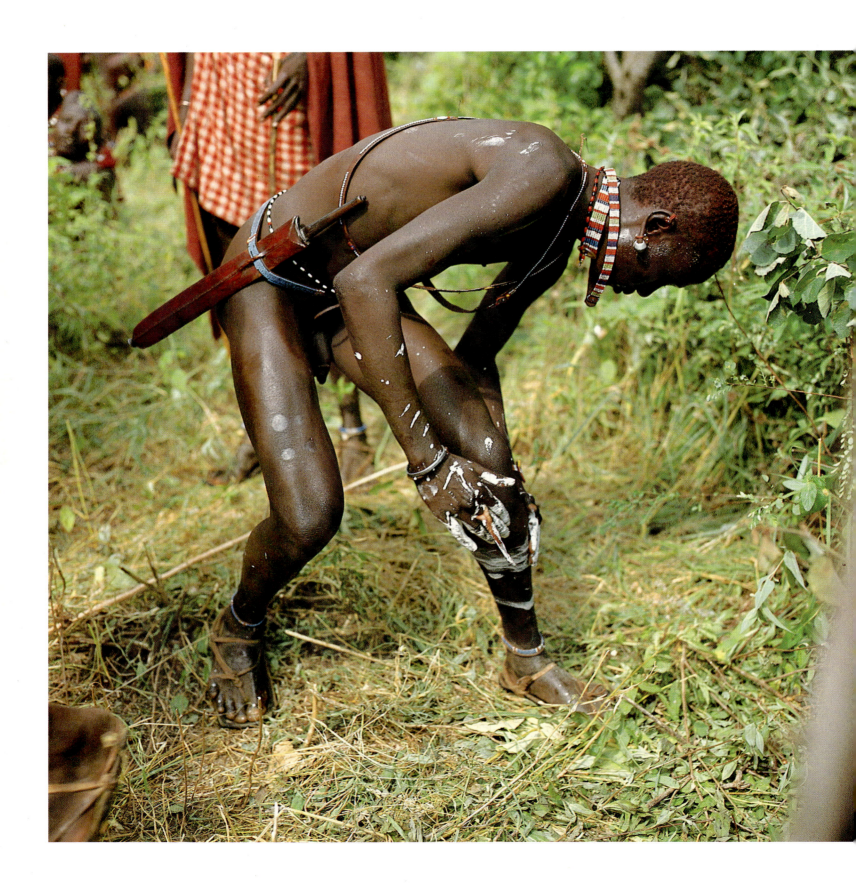

Below: Warriors tend the choice cuts from the sacrificial black ox.

elow: Choice cuts are broiled slowly over
mouldering fires of aromatic wood.

Below: Prized black bullock of the eunoto, *one of three, was donated by the father of one of three leaders of the moran. Black has significance as symbolic of good, or the benign side of the Maasai God, Enkai. It was the centrepiece of the* eunoto *feast, fattened up for days before on milk, honey-beer, and herbal mixtures supplied by the spiritual leader,* laibon. *When its throat is slit, the blood is mixed with milk and is sipped by all the moran in a form of communion conducted by the laibon and the senior elders.*

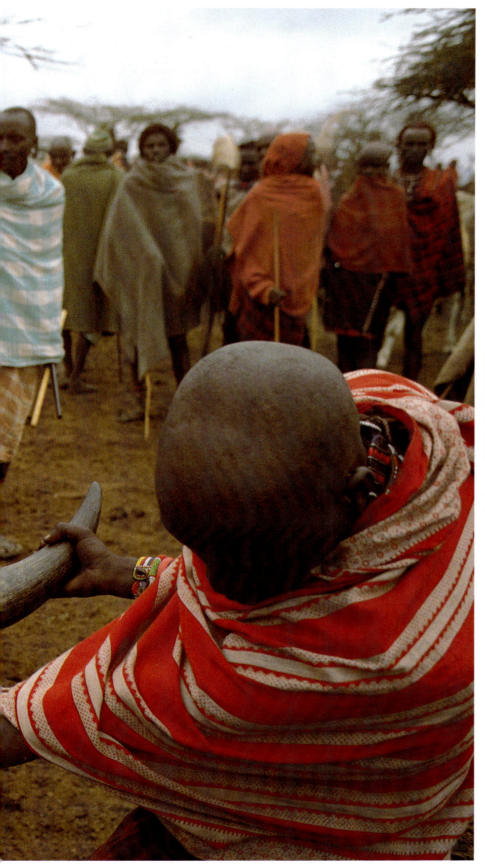

Above: The prime bull is ritually suffocated with a cloth, traditionally the skin skirt of a married woman.

Below: Ceremonially, the ritual experts of the
eunoto slit open the bull's dewlap and spread it
wide. The blood wells into the cavity into which milk
will be poured and then each candidate will drink
from the dewlap.

Opposite: Each moran takes his turn to sip the fres
blood.

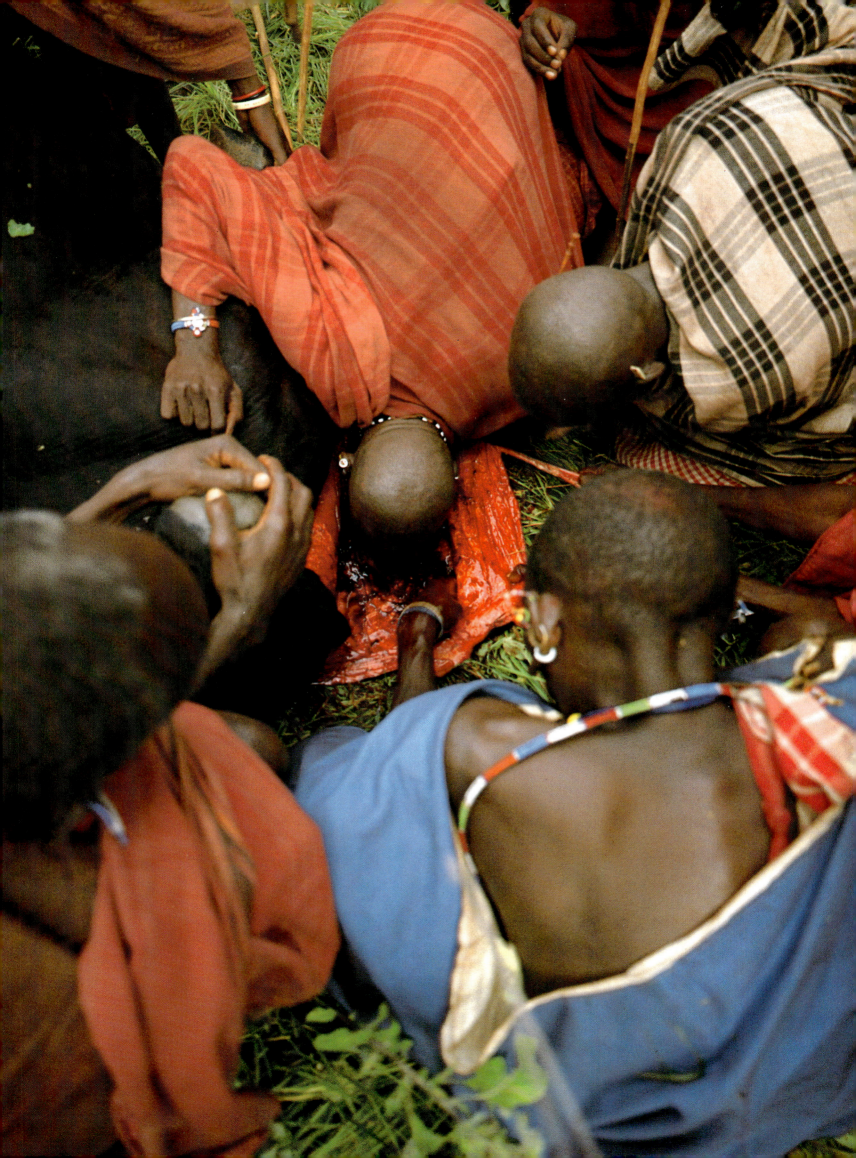

Opposite: Each part of the ox has its use in the
eunoto. An integral part of the ceremony is pegging
out the consecrated hide. This is performed by leading
matrons and matriarchs of the moran. Other women,
notably the adulterous ones, nkirekeny, are not
allowed to perform or witness this ritual. This
picture shows the il-piron elders preparing to cut
the hide into long strips from which the grafts will be
cut.

Below: Grafts of hide and sinew from the sacrificial
ox, here gathered on a spear, will be worn by all
eunoto graduates.

Opposite: Graduates line up to receive their strip of hide or sinew – the Maasai equivalent of the fraternity ring – as a token of their success in passing the judgement of the elders during the eunoto.

Below: More graduates, moran retiring to become junior elders, receive thongs of ox hide during the finale of the festival.

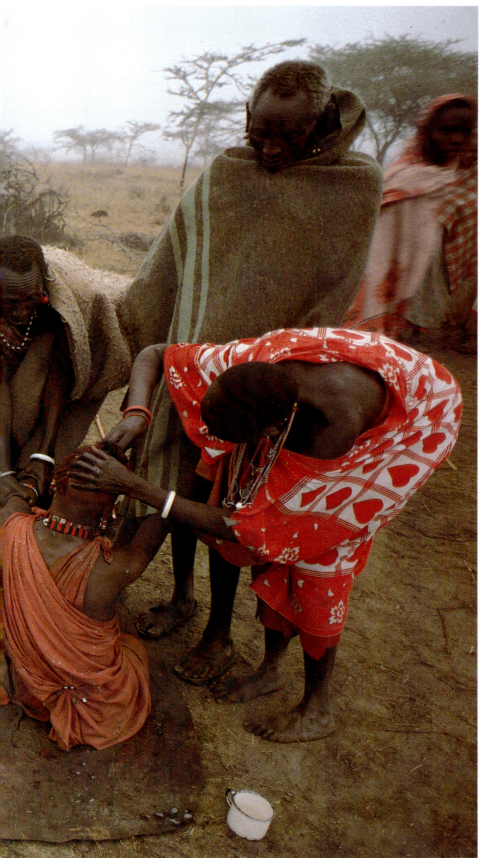

Left: Mothers shave the heads of their retiring warrior sons symbolically cutting the ties of warrior status, always painful to the egoistic dandies. Now the moran assume responsibilities of families and herds as junior elders.

Opposite: Weeping moran mourns the end of his elite warrior status as his cheerful mother prepares to shave his head for his entry into the ranks of the junior elders.

Below: Swiftly, the back of the head is stripped of its elaborate cockade, the front soon to follow.

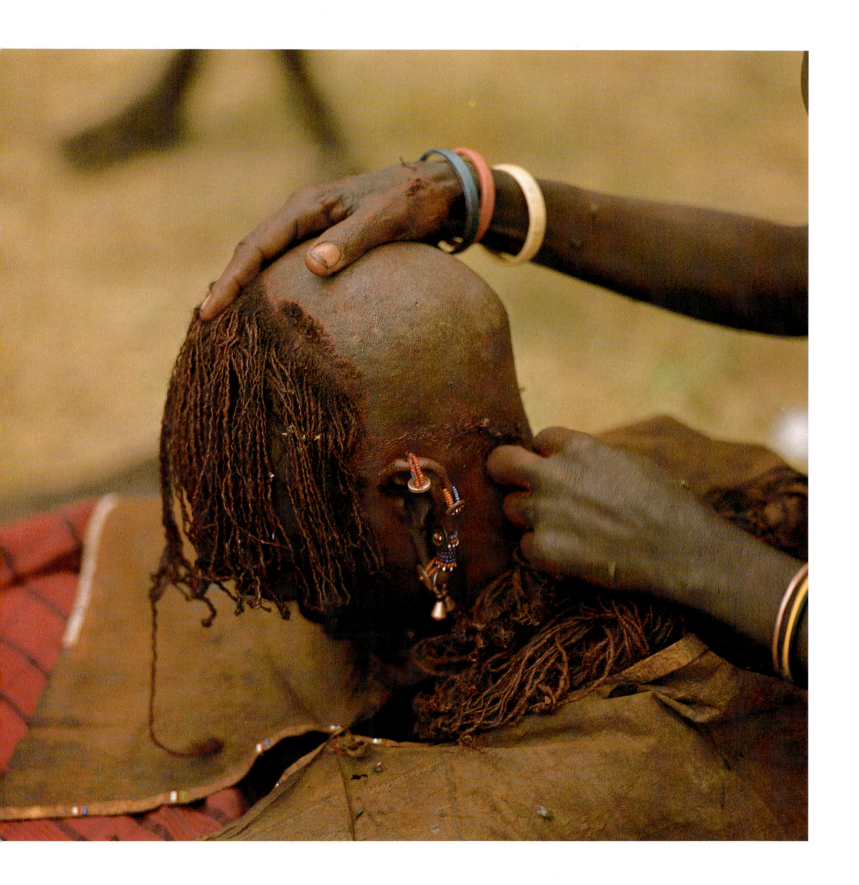

5

WOMANHOOD

Diana Kiremi, a young woman of the Il-Purko section, is by no means typical of the Maasai in Kajiado District where she was born. But she is expert and articulate on the life of Maasai women.

Her grandfather came from Mombasa, which suggests he may have been sold into slavery after the rout of the tribes by plague and famine in 1890. Her father was also 'different', having left the *manyatta* and started a small business in Bissel, a market village for beads, blankets and cloth on the road from Nairobi to Tanzania.

He sent Diana to a local mission school and afterwards to Nairobi University where she read education, literature and linguistics and graduated as the first woman Bachelor of Arts of the Maasai. She now collects and writes down Maasai lore before the traditions of her Il-Purko people disappear altogether in the tide of Bantu immigration across the Rift Valley border.

Her childhood was normal in the sense that she had her two lower incisor teeth taken out so that she could be fed in the event of lockjaw. She played with dolls made from a clay of laterite and cattle dung and learned the 'fairy tales' of the old women about the moran prince and the ogre.

From about the age of five – like all the other small girls of the settlement – she had to look after the calves, sheep and goats.

At 13, although the family had moved to the township at Bissel, she still went through the traditional rite of female circumcision, which normally involves the removal of the clitoris – sometimes the labia as well – in an operation that 'makes a child a woman'.

No one knows the origin of the practice nor sees any practical purpose in it. The Maasai offer no explanation, only that 'it is the custom', and apparently as ancient as the tribe itself. For the early missionaries, it was the worst abomination of the 'heathen'; the ultimate barbarity which they fought with such passion that it became a major issue for the Kikuyu, who may well have adopted the practice from the Maasai.

Diana's circumcision was carried out with less fuss than it would have been in a traditional *enkang*. Her head was shaved in the normal way, but then, instead of being the centre of attention of all the women of her family and clan, a relative slipped quietly into her house one night and performed a swift, unceremonious operation with a razor blade. Unlike the boys, no stoic silence is expected of the girls, and Diana screamed for all she was worth.

She talks about it without embarrassment. In answer to the question everyone asks, she says, 'there's a kind of sensory compensation elsewhere in the area'.

After the initiation by circumcision, a woman of the Maasai is allowed to marry through what is normally a 'social contract', arranged and

Previous page: Childhood passes swiftly for Maasai girls. Traditionally married in their teens, their prime duty is to produce sons to increase the father's prestige within the community.

executed by the girl's parents, the clan members, and sometimes the entire location.

'Everyone has a duty to get married,' Diana says. But occasionally a father will keep one or more of his daughters at home if he has no sons. The idea is that they will produce boys for him from men selected by her, which is important since women are not entitled to inherit their father's property in the patrilineal system.

Assuming a girl is free to leave home and marry, her women relatives begin casting around for a suitable husband. Blood relatives in the clan are rejected and so are members of her father's age-set since the 'blood brother' bonding at their initiation as warriors means that they are all 'father' to the girl and incest is taboo.

The method of betrothal is more or less the same in all sections, she says. What happens is that having spotted a girl for her son, the mother and one or two of her clanswomen visit her, carrying with them a piece of ornamental chain, a pat of butter or a handful of cow dung. They fuss over her and pretend to fix her ornaments and, in doing so, slip the chain over her head. They may also smear the butter and dung on her belly as a sign that they have an option on marrying her off to the man they represent. She may not guess immediately who this is, so the women will probably drop hints like: 'May you milk the cows of...' and then name the candidate's sub-clan. Eventually, the girl realises or finds out whom they are talking about and either accepts her fate or cleans off the marks on her stomach and throws away the 'betrothal chain'. She then has to get her father's approval for her rejection and his decision is final.

It could be that the girl has turned down the suitor because he is too old and decrepit, or too impoverished, or otherwise having trouble finding a wife. In this situation, Diana says, the man may be desperate enough to seduce a young uncircumcised girl and get her pregnant. The strategy is that her parents may then be persuaded to have her circumcised and married quickly to avoid further public disgrace. But in the old days, it seems that this would have been regarded as the girl's misbehaviour and an unforgivable and irredeemable offence against family honour. She might have been declared an outcast or, worse, taken into the bush, tied to a bull, and left for the hyaenas or for last-minute adoption by an individual or family in need of an extra workhand. Either way, her own family would never again have mentioned her name.

It happens occasionally that a girl avoids an arranged marriage by eloping with her boyfriend. But the usual consequence is that she is brought back by her brothers and beaten into submission. A rare exception was a girl who insisted she would marry the family's choice only if her eyes were 'plucked out so that she would never see his ugly face'. Apparently the speech and the tears were persuasive and thereafter arrangements were made among women matchmakers for her to marry her chosen lover in a series of ritual negotiations called in Maa, 'the beer that begets talk'.

The normal procedure – once all the talking is finished – is for the would-be groom to donate a heifer to the girl's father, a ewe to her mother, and a bull together with a cow and a calf as an assurance that the couple will produce children and so increase the family wealth. They might then be married immediately at a simple declaration of the event and a small party; or they could go through an elaborate ceremony that is a public holiday and barbecue for the entire community.

Among the preliminaries for this is the slaughter of two rams in celebration of shaving the head of the bride-to-be. Another sheep is killed and its fat stored for presentation to the groom later as a token of respect for his new wife. But the main pre-nuptial event is a traditional bachelor's night. The bride is invited and all the age-set 'fathers' lecture on the responsibilities of marriage. It's another occasion for a liberal flow of beer.

The following morning the girl is dressed in a bridal gown of leather, a profusion of beaded ornaments, and four leather rings made from the hide of the sacrificial sheep. She is also loaded down with symbols, including a calabash of milk, representing future prosperity. Four dolls are draped round her neck, three female and one male, which indicate the minimum number of children she might expect to produce. And she also wears slippers on the wrong feet to ward off evil.

The bride is then led in procession to what will be her personal gate in the circular thorn fence of the enclosure. She is blessed by two elders who take yet another fertility symbol of tied grass dipped in milk and honey-beer and anoint her face, body and feet. The text of the blessing could include 'may all your clan feed on you!' and 'may your back grow wide', presumably so that she can carry more children.

More fertility in the form of fresh grass is implanted in a leather girdle around her waist, and for some obscure reason also in her shoes. She is then ready to approach the matrimonial threshold, which she does in the company of four 'strangers' since her family and clansmen are not supposed to witness this ultimate act of surrender. Nor is she allowed to look back, only forward to a life of devotion to her new husband.

Her first steps towards this end are supervised by the 'best man' who sweeps a path clear for her and, if necessary, carries her over any river bed or gully. He must ensure that there is not the slightest obstacle in her way, so that there is no possibility of hesitation in her progress to the groom.

Eventually, safely delivered to the enclosure and welcomed with a gourd of fresh milk, she receives a gift of livestock from her new family.

Overleaf: Awaiting their turn for circumcision, a group of young girls in traditional dress and decoration, flanked by admiring intoyie. *The operation is usually performed by an invited 'practitioner' who is often not a Maasai, usually from a Dorobo group of hunter-gatherers, occasionally a Kikuyu. The knives and blades which make the cut are fashioned by blacksmiths,* il-kunono, *who are avoided by the Maasai because of their ritual impurity – they make weapons of death.*

On the third day the marriage is consummated. She cleanses herself first with a coat of red ochre and lies on a low cowhide bed for the first performance of what will be a frequent duty. The main stress in her life from then on is over the number of children she can produce, which is never quite enough. If there are no signs of pregnancy, the anxiety builds up until all the women get together for mass psychotherapy in a ceremony called 'the holy gathering'. Father Mol once saw this event in Loita District, with more than 800 women taking part. The rituals centred around a tree whose thick white sap was considered a potent maternity symbol for its similarity to mother's milk.

When a woman does become pregnant, she is indulged with tender loving care, except that the husband cannot demonstrate his feelings sexually in case the act loosens the tie between mother and embryo and causes a miscarriage. She may not be given meat from an animal that has died naturally for fear it might infect or otherwise damage the unborn child. In any event, the woman is given less protein than usual and more carbohydrates to help towards an easier delivery.

Father Mol remarked on the careful cosseting of a Maasai mother after her confinement. She is first of all 'in a state of grace', an expression which derives from the verb 'to beseech' and implies that the new mother has been pious and eloquent enough in her prayers to be 'favoured of God'.

She is excused all heavy work, such as the pre-dawn milking and the evening collection of firewood, which is either taken over by her husband's other wives or by a younger sister assigned to her from the parental home. She is further preserved from strain by an extension of the ban on sexual relations, which in effect keeps her husband away from the start of the pregnancy until the child is weaned.

The incidence of infant mortality is high among the Maasai and a baby is not truly recognised until it has survived at least three 'moons', *ilapaitin*. Thereafter, it is given a name in a simple family ceremony at which the head of the child is shaved clean apart from a tuft of hair like a cock's comb from the forehead to the nape of the neck. If, in a previous pregnancy, the mother had lost a child, the hair would be positioned at the front or the back of the head, depending on whether the dead infant had been a boy or a girl.

In some communities, the father takes no apparent interest in his child until it is toddling around; but elsewhere both parents are demonstrative in showing affection to their babies.

posite: Female circumcision initiates. First of the

es of passage for Maasai girls, the ceremony which
ese white-painted youngsters undergo is a ritual
eration marking their transition to womanhood.

Below: Newly circumcised girls hide their face as
custom decrees.

Overleaf: Maasai moran with his mother.

6

DILEMMA

In the forest of the Loita Hills is a cathedral of seven old trees. This is unmarked except when the Maasai are there in communion with their remote God, *Enkai*. The circle of trees is then defined by bunches of grass, the ancient insignia for truce or sanctuary. They call the place 'where the grass is tied', *Naemi-Nkujit*.

A retreat to the hills usually follows trouble of some kind. In the old days it was civil war, or disease and famine, or an ordinary cyclic drought which burned the lowland grazing to grey ash. But today, it might also start from a burgeoning town on the Loita Plains called Narosura.

To the pastoral Maasai out on the plains, the place is a spectre of change, a market without cattle, a settlement without tribal community. It is final dereliction in two rows of scrap iron stores, which provide hardly more than shade for the resident Maasai who wander from one shack to the next, touching fingertips, spitting and talking. They appear to buy nothing in the market, and specifically nothing from a Bantu street-trader offering more of the new, 'civilised' life style in a pile of cast off cotton dresses and trousers.

A few old men in ochred rags squat in the dust of a garage driveway playing an endless game with pebbles and a wooden board like an egg tray. Other lethargic groups are children in the middle of the street where flies settle on their eyes or on milk scum around their mouths. There is, in fact, nothing unusual in this tolerance of flies, which are always too numerous and persistent to fend off. But there's also a more fundamental lassitude among the Maasai of Narosura.

The way out, if they choose to take it, is along a new road to the hills, which dips into a small river at the edge of town and then glints away in a straight line to the distant wall of a high escarpment. It then follows an old footpath alignment, with the road hung on the face of the mountain like a loose thread. Sometimes it disappears in folds of olive forest but then reappears twisted around outcrops of rock or pulled taut up the side of a cliff.

A few elders remember the climb, before the road, as a kind of Via Dolorosa to the holy place beyond the summit. They describe an exhausting and fearful journey, with the sunlight shut out by the thickleaf canopy of the trees and the path wet, slippery and cut in places by encroaching bush.

They moved in single file, with a silent and frightened cluster of women following behind, wary of wild animals but more nervous of the benign or malevolent 'Spirit of God'. They were never sure which because *Enkai* is imagined essentially in two colours – as a mythical compassionate 'Black God' or vengeful 'Red God'. The Maasai deity is also imagined as 'multicoloured', which is how the Maasai explain *Enkai*'s infinite, formless variety and capricious treatment of humans.

But talk of God would be taboo on the Narosura escarpment because any question on the nature of the Almighty would lack respect. But once over the rim of the scarp and into the soft hills of the Loita, the Maasai might discuss the nature of the 'Holy Land', which would be in a combination of colours, but mostly 'black' for good, and sacred.

In European tourist prose, the scenery is to some extent reminiscent of home, or it was to one traveller: 'We came out to an alpine valley whose immense rolling plains, shining in the setting sun seemed as smooth as a golf course. But this was at once shattered by the sight of some russet impala that came out of a grove to stare at us. The grove was also something which seemed to belong to another world, for the bunched trees looked like English holly with their dark green leaves now burnished in the sun. Then, on all the surrounding ridges, we saw great stands of deep cedar forest and, like small islands on the vivid green plains, the painted herds of the laibon's cattle. It was a strikingly beautiful scene.'

It was almost certainly the 'valley of the laibons' near a small settlement called Entasekera. But the description also fits other natural parks in this remote, mysterious, infinite sweep of 'God's country' across the Tanzanian border to the high plains of the Serengeti.

One range of hills in the Loita is a dark, sinister wood in local folklore. The area is still called 'where the little girl was lost', *Naimina-enkiyio*. The nursery lesson that inspired the name is buried in obscurity but the cultural historian of the Loita, Father Frans Mol, wrote it down and his translation retains the original simplicity and colour of the Maa language:

'The little girl, who felt so glad that the great *Enkai* had made her a Maasai, went out one glorious morning to herd her father's calves. But, straying further and further, curious as most small girls would be and a little afraid as well, she entered the forbidding forest above her father's village. Once more she looked back and saw the familiar bluish smoke curling from her mother's house; her little brother, Leteipa, toddling behind the sheep and goats; and the wide, wide land of Loita at her golden feet, rolling endlessly across the hills to the horizon. Then she turned again and went on into the forest.

'Later, when the sun had sunk behind the ridges of Osoit Sampu and seemed to burn itself out over the Serengeti, the calves returned home without their little shepherdess. Warriors were sent at once to search for her and called her name amid the darkening trees, at first confident and casual, but gradually in desperation and sadness until their voices faded away into history. The forest never gave her back; a little girl lost in a forest where, even today, men fear to go.'

Most of the trees in the area of the legend are 'cold', which means they are without thorns, and some of them are sacred. The 'cathedral' of seven fig trees is not far away, but hidden from 'profane eyes' unless the processional way is marked with the sheaves of grass. During a prayer service, these are tied, untied and retied over and again in a ritual symbolising a renewal of the bonds between the supplicants and God.

The prayers themselves are sung in a kind of a litany, with the laibon or a venerable elder leading and the congregation calling out responses such as:
Naai tadamu iyiook!
Oh God, remember us!

Although *Enkai* is not imagined in human form and no images are made, this spirit is sometimes invested with bodily parts, with the Maasai making solemn requests for protection under his armpits or in his navel. But mostly, their prayer is common and universal:

Oh God, grant that we may live in peace.
Give us health,
And protect our wives and children.
Bless us with rain on our heads,
And prosper us by giving water to man and beast.'
Naai tadamu iyiook!
God, remember us!

The Maasai tend to address the Almighty individually and in private. The one time they will get together for community prayers is at the low point of a ten-year cycle of prosperity and disaster which is so regular and predictable they have a word for it, *ol-ngaeitai*.

In the old days, they would pray for recovery after disease or drought or defeat in war. Today, they pray over the image of Narosura town, the degrading alternative to the freedoms of their pastoral system. The disaster, as they see it, is a disruptive combination of political pressure for cultural change, enforced settlement, loss of cattle and loss of land to immigrant cultivators.

The Maasai have a religious aversion to agriculture. *Enkai* prohibits it for true Maasai. It is alien to their culture and they have suffered from its effects ever since the British planted the first wheat in the Mau highlands. They despise the 'diggers of the earth'; but they can do very little about them moving into the fertile, 'high potential' areas of Maasailand, burning out the forest, and hand-hoeing the black soil into patches of maize, potatoes and beans.

The Bantu farmers push forward into what are often vital dry-weather retreats for the nomad Maasai, who are then confined to the dry lowland range. In a year of good rains, there may be enough grazing. But in the ten-year cyclic drought, the stock losses are high, and not infrequently the Maasai are reduced to subsistence on imported cereals.

The result is trauma. Much as they are emotionally attached to the earth, their roots are aerial and symbiotic with the free-ranging cattle. Any variation of their diet of meat and milk, or any reduction of their mobility, tends to cause a profound reaction. They may become aggressive or apathetic, reacting to what they feel is a loss of identity.

One issue, a few years ago, was the declared intention of the Kenya Government to take over all the Maasai highlands for 'national water conservation projects', which eventually, the Maasai suspected, would be used for growing more cereals and beans. The Maasai opposed the proposal on the basis of their own accounting of the Mau wheat scheme, which shows they were generally robbed by sharecroppers and relieved of essential wetlands – for no return whatsoever to the local communities of Maasai.

An alternative reaction, of passive decline and sell out, is evident all along the Rift Valley border and around Mount Meru and Mount Kilimanjaro in Tanzania. The detail of the story of capitulation and displacement changes from place to place, but the basic scenario is written in an American journalist's report of graduated change around Loitokitok on the Kenya-Tanzania border.

He describes a sundown on Kilimanjaro, with 'the darkness creeping down the forested lower slopes, sliding across fields of maize, finally reaching the thorn trees and short yellow flatlands where the sons of a traditional Maasai elder are herding the cattle into the *enkang* for the night'.

The old man watches them come in, reflecting on the toll of a recent drought which reduced his walking wealth from about 1,000 to 150 head of cattle. Many died, he told the reporter, and the rest were bartered for maize from a half-Maasai, half-Bantu neighbour down the road who was evidently not a great deal happier with life than the elder. The neighbour regretted his progress to mixed farming and even rejected the Bantu half of his personality.

'We Maasai,' the elder said, 'have always moved where there is grass and water, but now we must stay where we are. The government wants centres of settlement, schools and so forth, and has given us farms. But the land that used to be enough for the Maasai is now shared with others, and we have to rely on the government to bring in water. The land is drying all round.'

He made a particular gesture to the next farm down the road to Loitokitok where a resettled Bantu was ploughing a field of dry grass. A plume of dust trailed his tractor, but the ploughman was unconcerned. He thought the rains would probably come as usual to grow his crops. If not, he agreed that maybe the topsoil of his twelve acres of Maasailand would blow away altogether. In which case he would have to move on.

The story is typical of the insidious erosion of Maasailand. According to their own government of elders, it is a deliberate offensive against the Maasai, and also a mindless repetition of the policy 'agricultural is right, pastoral is wrong'. There may be an argument for grabbing arable land in the hills, the elders say, but ploughing up the fragile lowland is a cynical exchange of short-term political profit for long-term dust.

The elders still insist that every acre of the Tribal Trust land is part of an inalienable, freehold estate of the people of Maa collectively. But this ignores the government's formal subdivision of the land and the issue of titles.

The settled Maasai are also targets of the main thrust of government pressure for social and economic reform. The demand at official meetings is for them to work ranches, produce beef and pay taxes. They are invited to apply for loans to upgrade their stock and pasture and are urged to diversify into dairy and crop production – including, at one stage, the cropping of stray wildlife on a 'sustained yield basis'. From the net income, it is put forth, they can support themselves and their cattle through any period of drought and finance their own social development in the construction of schools, health facilities and commercial enterprises.

In general, the Maasai response is to listen with what is described as polite but phenomenal disinterest. They may join with the developers in long and serious discussion, agree to some progressive action or other, and thereafter do precisely nothing.

This stubborn, passive resistance appears to bemuse their appointed politicians in the national parliament and in the district councils. They advocate radical change among the Maasai but at the same time are conservative and defensive. A published statement by one of these politicians is typical:

'The puerile imputations that the Maasai are lazy people and are kept alive by their wives, or are parasites, are essentially infra-dig,' wrote the ministerial representative of Narok District. 'To begin with, the Maasai are a warrior race of international renown who could not possibly be kept by their wives, except in the sense that women are universally necessary for the propagation of the tribe, as well as for other obvious feminine consolations and benefits.'

He suggested that anyone who expressed contempt for the Maasai did so 'because their forefathers might have had occasion to feel the business end of a spear'.

'These people will never drive the Maasai from their land,' he wrote. 'It was not given to them on a silver platter, but bought with the blood of our ancestors. Anybody with a rudimentary knowledge of the history of Kenya knows that we were deprived of our best land to make way for white settlement. It is true that with the advent of *Uhuru* (Independence) the white settlers are more or less gone. It is equally true that the people who are now being resettled on our land are not Maasai, but our fellow *wananchi* (citizens). We are not complaining about this new development, but the Maasai most certainly expect, and in fact demand, that no one should be so greedy as to cast envious eyes on the mostly dry crumbs of land on which we are now struggling to eke out an existence. The land has always been – and will continue to be – defended by true Maasai blood.'

An attempt was also made to defend it politically with the reformation of a defunct party organisation, the Maasai United Front (MUF). This was originally formed before Independence to 'safeguard Maasai institutions' and because of 'an increasing concern that surrounding tribes desire to move in and take control of the land; and that they possess the physical force and technical knowledge to do so'.

Not surprisingly, the revival of a nuisance group of Maasai was disallowed and that included the apolitical 'cultural and social' organisation suggested for the new MUF. The policy, as the British Commissioner Sir Charles Eliot first proposed, 'is to change their peculiar ideas and break up their organisation'.

The obvious first target for this is the moran system. Every *eunoto* graduation is officially declared to be the last and once, in 1973, the system was actually proscribed by government order. 'War-songs' and 'war-cries' were banned and, for a while, a dusk-to-dawn curfew was imposed. The Maasai were told to do away with the *manyatta*s and send the warriors to school, or forfeit their cattle in fines.

The decree was never enforced, but the public debate on the 'outdated, lawless, useless' warrior system continues. The politicians respond and the elders maintain their silent, inactive defence against imposed change.

Sometimes the government manages to harry them into at least making a start on land reform. But rank outsiders like the United Nations development agencies tend to come and go with their 'range management' and 'wildlife utilisation' schemes without leaving any obvious impression on the Maasai or the land.

One 'beneficial' and unwanted project in Kajiado District was a US$3 million demonstration of how to slaughter wildlife and market the meat. As usual the elders were prepared to take part in meetings, but not in the project – which they rejected for 'ethical reasons'.

The same Kajiado Maasai blocked the private initiative of a local wildlife society to expand Nairobi National Park. They staged what amounted to a 'settle-in' on the land which was being sold off at three dollars an acre. The clients, mostly Americans, bought honorary title to a piece of 'wild Africa' and immediately handed over the deeds to the park authorities and posterity.

The Maasai were eventually consulted and they agreed to move out so long as they were given an equivalent area of land in Kikuyu or Kamba country and were fully compensated for the loss of cattle dips, schools and dispensaries they were busily setting up. The scheme was quietly shelved.

Their more general case against erosion of land rights by tourism was once articulated by a senior age-set leader of the Il-Kisonko division, Edward ole Mbarnoti.

'It is we Maasai who have preserved this priceless heritage in our land. We were sharing it with the wild animals long before the arrival of those who use game only as a means of making money. So please do not tell us that we must be pushed off our land for the financial convenience of commercial hunters and hotel-keepers. Nor tell us that we must live only by the rules and regulations of zoologists.' And then perhaps broadening the appeal: 'If Uhuru means anything at all, it means that we are to be treated like humans, not animals.'

The argument persists. The Maasai claim that the last great and profitable wildlife range in Africa would not exist but for the fact that they are traditionally able to live in harmony with nature. So why, they ask, should they be excluded from national parks which are, by definition, feudal and anti-social – 'like hunting grounds in England before the Magna Carta, where only the aristocrats could hunt and where the peasants are persecuted'.

They suggested that a more sensible policy, in line with the post-colonial constitution of Kenya, would be to remove the armed guards from the parks and restore the natural order, with wild animals and Maasai working out the water and grazing allocations themselves. The implication is that it would be a fair share-out – but some doubt is expressed, among others by the noted ecologist, Sir Frank Fraser-Darling. He agreed that 'traditionally, the Maasai disdained to hunt anything but an occasional predator for sport or in retribution for stock-killing. Since there was no cultivation, there was no antipathy towards wild ruminants for the damage they might cause; and since the Maasai are nutritionally self-sufficient with their herds and flocks, they are not hunters. But neither are they philanthropists and they look with some longing and probable anticipation at the grazing potential of large, virgin areas which will eventually be cleared of the tsetse fly.'

Someone once proposed monuments to the Maasai and the tsetse fly in recognition of their joint contribution to wildlife conservation. But, as Fraser-Darling wrote as early as 1960, 'the needling which veterinary science and benign government have made available is turning the Maasai against the game. There is now competition, not so much for grazing as for water; and where there is competition, there is attrition – and the game animals are on the losing side.

'It remains to be seen how much wildlife will be lost as a result of the radically changed attitudes of the Maasai, the more intensive pastoralism and land degeneration, and African gang poaching – the senseless killing by Africans under a halfhearted or uninformed government policy professing care.'

As it turned out, the destruction of wildlife in a short period in the early seventies was incalculable. The extent of the die-off is merely indicated in a set of figures produced by a group of United Nations experts in Kajiado. They were there to conserve wildlife, or to produce protein from it – no one is sure which – and they estimated that between 75 and 85 per cent of plains game were wiped out by a combination of poaching, overgrazing and drought.

The local moran were seen to make a contribution, poaching freely at one stage under the patronage of a few politicians in Nairobi and Narok, who came to regard the game as a bank-in-kind for the support of the new progressive life style. The moran also speared a few animals as a political protest, most effectively at Amboseli where they removed almost all the rhino in response to their exclusion from the only permanent water in the area.

This kind of demonstration would not be necessary, they suggest, if all wild and domestic stock in Maasailand were to be assigned to the management of the Maasai. If this just and enlightened policy were to be adopted, they could guarantee positive self-development. As a designated State Conservation Area, Maasailand would cease to be a national liability and finally become half-way independent in the nation-state of Kenya.

Epilogue

The road from Nairobi to the Loita Hills ends at the top of the Narosura escarpment. From there on, motorised traffic tends to get bogged down or run up against dead ends on meandering cattle tracks. The country is mostly wild and so, by the look of them, are the Il-Loita Maasai.

There is no restriction on stock movement; no settlement schemes they need pay any great attention to; and, perversely, the government of elders is promoting what the national government would call 'significant progress'. It was once thought that this might be imposed on them: in the 1950s when the British colonial authorities deemed the area suitable for immigration, clearance and crop production. The idea was dropped after an engineer commissioned for 'a final and complete hydrological survey' fell off a rock and sprained an ankle. He returned to Nairobi and reported that there was insufficient water for agriculture in the Loita Hills.

The Maasai were further amused a few years later when a Dutch priest arrived at an *enkang* location called Il-kerin looking for permanent water on which to found the first Christian Catholic mission to the Loita. He reported on his reception to the presiding Bishop of the Maasailand Diocese.

'It was April, the fly season; the cows had just come back to the *enkang* from the plains. The women were milking and an old man sat enjoying the evening sun. Hordes of flies were swarming around, unbearably irritating to one unused to their savage and continual attacks. But the old man was unconcerned, fanning the insects away with a slow shoulder-to-shoulder movement of a whisk made from the tail of a giraffe – ''the-one-whose-sleeping-is-long''.

'We ate the news together', as the Maasai say; and when this ceremony was completed, he began to chuckle. His merriment was such that I imagined he was very old indeed.

'Presently he said: ''So you're the one trying to find water here at Il-kerin?''

'I said I was.

'''Could I not be your father?''

'''You could'', I replied.

'''Well then, boy, go home. If we have failed to find it in a lifetime, and others before us in theirs, then how can you succeed in a day or two? There is no water at Il-kerin,'' he said and laughed again.'

Some time later, after this initial survey, construction started on the first of two large earth dams that were to greatly impress the Il-Loita Maasai. The impossible mission began to work, then expanded over ten years, to become a modern 3,000-acre ranch, dairy farm and general education complex.

The story is told mostly in files of project statistics, but the more significant information is in a trace of human reaction and incident in a footnote commentary on the figures. Sometimes their frustration in dealing with the 'cussed and arrogant' Maasai overrides the priestly restraint, but in their generally patient handling of the elders is an indication of what could be a future process of change among the rearguard conservative majority.

The priests' technique is gentle persuasion by example; by manipulating the Maasai's supreme interest in themselves and in owning bigger and better cattle; and by allowing the council of elders to come in to run the project itself in its own elegant style of perhaps a week's debate for a simple management decision. The procedure is not exactly efficient, but it moves the Maasai slowly forward from mild amusement, disdain or disinterest to curiosity, selective acceptance of development and gradual change within the traditional system.

The starting point at Il-kerin was open-minded interest and a degree of humility, which immediately set the project apart from most other private, government, United Nations and missionary enterprises in Maasailand. The priests got to know the people affected, learned their language and listened. This way, they were at least able to appreciate the simple facts of Maasai life as they set about changing it.

They learned first that the Maasai understand cattle and are experts in animal husbandry and range management. They know every blade of grass in the neighbourhood and the general ecological variations of the communal range: its stock carrying capacity, its seasonal yields in pasture and water, and its efficient use in an established pattern of rotation grazing. Each group of families is keyed into this pattern, and the economic or life-support system breaks down if and when the communities are obliged to claim exclusive title to land within the tribal territory.

The ancient practice of one community ceding grazing to the next when necessary is further reinforced by the age-set system and its unbreakable pacts of brotherly love and understanding. This is why, in practice, the idea of breaking up northern Maasailand into private or group ranches is largely a failure and why, in theory, the collective farm idea in Tanzania could work if sensibly applied.

The Fathers at Il-kerin understand all this; that there can be no fences in Maasailand and no settled, subordinate Maasai before some kind of revolution replaces the age-set system with a new order and ideology.

They accept that, for the present, the Maasai are not to be governed, employed or managed, nor even worked with, on equal terms. Like all politicians in Maasailand, the priests exert influence only from the back bench in the traditional Maasai government, through influence with the age-set leaders in council. In their novel – and in many ways model – democracy, the Fathers are persuasive and in effect are accepted as consultant vets, stockmen, salesmen and bankers. The result is tangible change in the life of the Il-Loita Maasai, not only within the boundaries of the project but also outside.

The Maasai are coming in for the permanent water in the dams, for advice and services, and to admire the improved stock at the ranch. They also sell cattle occasionally which are then walked a hundred miles to a government buyer.

No one would claim that everything works at Il-kerin, nor that the movement of the Maasai towards fuller participation in national life is indicated by anything much – except that they do have a new prayer to Enkai:

Naai,
Intamelono nintorropil enyamali nikinyamalaki
Ti atua il-oshon oo-tii
Ena murua naya sipili
Naai,
Incoo iyiook nintobikoo
Mataa erishina oreteti memetoyu
Ti atua olameyu le kujit
Ntarasi e kishon o kishon
Naai tadamu iyiook

Oh God,
Bring sweetness and fragrance
To the troubles with which we are bothered
Among the lives of our people and of the country;
And,
Oh God,
Give us the strength to do the work we have started here
At our Il-kerin home,
The spearhead of a force that, we pray, Will hold out like the oreteti tree
That never dries even in drought.
Let it be so for the Maasai of today
And for generations to come.
Oh God, remember us!